A Leader's Guide to

FIGHTING INVISIBLE TIGERS

A Stress Management Guide for Teens

12 Sessions on Stress Management and Lifeskills Development

Connie C. Schmitz, Ph.D., with Earl Hipp

free spirit
PUBLiSHiNG®

Works
for kids®

ISBN 0-915793-81-4

Table 2: "Gender Differences in Assets, Deficits, and At-Risk Behavior" on page 14 is from Benson, Peter L. (1993). *The Troubled Journey: A Portrait of 6th–12th Grade Youth.* Search Institute and the Lutheran Brotherhood, Minneapolis (MN), p. 61. Used with permission.

Cover and book design by MacLean & Tuminelly
Edited by Pamela Espeland
Index prepared by Eileen Quam and Theresa Wolner

15 14 13 12 11 10 9 8 7
Printed in the United States of America

Free Spirit Publishing Inc.
217 Fifth Avenue North, Suite 200
Minneapolis, MN 55401-1299
(612) 338-2068
help4kids@freespirit.com
www.freespirit.com

ACKNOWLEDGMENTS

We'd like to thank several people for guiding us as we researched materials for this revision. Dr. Kate Donaldson, a licensed psychologist who works in private practice with adolescents and families, pointed the way to some useful texts and served as a reviewer of these materials. Kate Kalb at the Minnesota State Health Department (Division of Adolescent Health) was informative in guiding us to sources for recent national statistics. Dr. Michael Resnick of the University of Minnesota Division of General Pediatrics and Adolescent Health provided us with several reports on adolescent stress that are noted throughout the book. We are also indebted to Dr. Dale Blythe of Search Institute in Minneapolis for sending us relevant materials. Despite their kind help, these folks should not be blamed for any unintentional errors or inaccuracies on our part; the opinions and suggestions offered in this book (unless noted) come from us, and we remain responsible for them.

For those of you who use these materials, we wish you well. We'd also like to hear back from you how things went—what worked well for you and what didn't. On page 126 there is a "Leader's Guide Evaluation" with a list of questions. We would appreciate your responses. Whether you teach all or just some of the sessions, feel free to write to us in care of Free Spirit Publishing Inc., 217 Fifth Avenue North, Suite 200, Minneapolis, MN 55401-1299.

Connie C. Schmitz
Earl Hipp

Just Friends Bookclub

This Book Belongs to:

V. Pat Mott

CONTENTS

LIST OF REPRODUCIBLE PAGES

INTRODUCTION

Before the discovery of antibiotics in the early part of the 20th century, the primary health problems that Americans faced were biological. Infectious diseases were the big childhood killers, and highest mortality rates in the population were found among the young. A walk through a turn-of-the-century cemetery illustrates this reality with a startling poignancy: so many gravestones for so many little children and infants.

Today the situation is quite different. The highest mortality rates can be found among the elderly, and our primary health problems are no longer biological in nature but psychosocial and behavioral. To be sure, AIDS is a major health threat with a biological basis, but its control rests largely on social and behavioral factors. Poisonous chemicals are infiltrating the earth's water, air, ground, food, housing, etc., and our genetic inheritance still sets the stage for certain incapacities. But many of the most prevalent illnesses and health problems today (such as heart disease, lung cancer, domestic abuse, handgun violence, and addictions to tobacco, alcohol, and other drugs) can no longer be explained by the "medical model" alone. The connections between health and lifestyle, discretionary behaviors, stress, and the emotions are being increasingly recognized and understood.[1] Contemporary dangers, it has been said, are no longer physical in origin so much as psychological.[2]

For teenagers, stress has both an internal and external component. First, teens have the "normal" stress of growing up. This includes the developmental tasks of growing physically, mentally, and emotionally, and making all the psychological adjustments that entails. Growing up means figuring out how to separate from parents and clarify just who one is in relation to family and peer groups. It means experiencing sexuality and new relationships. But in addition to this "normal" stress, we must add the stresses of living in contemporary American culture. This means:

- Living in a violent society, in which (in an average month) 43% of black teenage males and 41% of white teenage males will have carried a weapon.[3]

- A steadily increasing teen violent death rate: 69.3 deaths per 100,000 teens in 1989, which represented a 11% increase over the previous five years.[4] Perhaps this is why, in 1994, the Centers for Disease Control and Prevention identified handgun violence as the nation's number one public health risk.

- A worsening juvenile custody rate: 156 teens per 100,000 for kids aged 10–15 in 1989, which represented a 10% increase over a four-year period.[5]

- Living with divorced or separated parents. Approximately one-quarter of all children and adolescents in the United States lived in single-parent homes between 1987–91.[6]

- Having to find one's way in the world, despite the loss of neighborhood and community support systems, eroding religious institutions and public schools. Public schools are especially under siege and increasingly unable to help many students learn. Academic underachievement for high school boys in particular is believed to be extremely common: estimates have run as high as 30% to 40% of all adolescent males.[7]

- Growing up in a changing economy in which unemployment and underemployment for youth and young adults has essentially extended adolescence until the late twenties.

- Being confronted with unrestricted freedoms and access to extremely negative influences. Those influences include everything from the sexuality on the television, to the violence in schools, to rampant materialism, to negative peer groups, to the drug pusher on the street corner.

Psychologists like David Elkind who work with adolescents believe that our culture no longer provides youth with a safe transition period in which to grow and develop.[8] These large societal influences affect all teens, indirectly if not directly. And we know that some teens, by accident of birth and subsequent racism, classism, and sexism, are especially prone to emotional stress. This includes teens of color, teens in poverty, and girls in general.[9,10] Once regarded as a safe haven, the midwestern rural town now logs alarming statistics for binge drinking (followed by driving) and teen suicide. Rural adolescents, it has been found, "drink more often and drink in greater quantity than urban teenagers."[11]

Is it getting harder and harder to grow up in American society? Some people say it is. We've always been suspicious of the nostalgic picture drawn of the 1950s as a kind of stress-free heaven for kids. We don't think earlier times were necessarily all that kinder or gentler for all kids. Yet, while we don't think the past is ever as good as we sometimes make it out to be, we do feel that today's teenagers face a complicated task in coming of age in the United States.

To say that it is important to teach lifeskills to teens is an understatement. Each year in this country, more than 40,000 young people die from preventable causes—primarily car crashes, homicides, suicides, and other accidents.[12] In an average year, one in ten adolescent females will attempt suicide.[13] While the leading cause of death for white teens is automobile crashes (usually associated with alcohol use), the leading cause of death for black adolescent males is homicide.[14] Teenage pregnancy, school drop-outs, violent injuries, running away from home, drug and alcohol abuse, anorexia and bulimia, self-mutilation—are all serious problems that have been escalating over the past decades.

The ideas and tools provided in this book won't prevent all of the mental, physical, and emotional threats to teen health, but lifeskills may make it easier for teens to survive. Just helping them to become aware of the stressors in their lives, and providing them with a setting where it is okay to talk about stress and talk about ways to "get it together," may be the biggest gifts you can give them. It is our hope that this book will arm you with a few more ways to work the prevention side of the street with teens who are still in class, still coming to youth meetings at church or other groups. It may give you, the teacher or youth leader, a stronger commitment

to teach the affective side of education, when budget cuts and back-to-basics proponents threaten any subject other than English, math, or science.

If you've already read Earl Hipp's book, *Fighting Invisible Tigers: A Stress Management Guide for Teens,* many of the concepts presented here on stress and stress management will be familiar to you. For those of you unfamiliar with the term "lifeskills," we define it as an assortment of stress-reducing, life-enhancing strategies that keep people feeling emotionally and physically balanced. In a well-adjusted adult (or young person), lifeskills show up as a rather personal collection of health or lifestyle habits, attitudes, beliefs, and behaviors. The lifeskills presented in these materials are not all-encompassing by any means, but as a group they do touch on diverse areas (i.e., physical, mental, social), they are solidly grounded in principles related to stress management, and they do work!

Lifeskills are rarely taught in a straightforward manner in our culture, particularly to young adults. When they are discussed in school, they're typically addressed inadvertently or in piecemeal style through courses in the "regular" curriculum. For instance, students can learn the biological facts of stress, nutrition, body chemistry, physical growth and development in health and science courses. In another corner of the school, communication skills (i.e., rhetoric) may be taught in speech class, or practiced in drama class, or the student council—but rarely do such courses deal with the kind of interpersonal communication skills that promote supportive relationships. For upper-class students, personal goal-setting might be encouraged in individual career counseling sessions. After school, opportunities for physical exercise abound in multiple sports activities. For many students, however, competitive school athletics have the opposite effect of a supportive lifeskill or relaxation strategy. Some in-school counseling or support groups may deal with personal goals, values, and "self-talk," but these groups are typically designed to treat students after problems have occurred, and are not available to all young people on a prevention basis.

While all of these courses and activities contain information that's useful to the development of lifeskills, it's up to the individual to make the connections—to pull it together in a meaningful fashion.

Usually, the information supplied is superficial at best, or presented so indirectly that students fail to personalize the concepts. Similarly, the amount of time commonly allowed for practicing lifeskills is inadequate, so few of the behaviors suggested are actually implemented or maintained after the course concludes.

In contrast, these materials reflect an interdisciplinary approach. The psychobiology of stress and stress management skills form the thematic center of the course, and each of the twelve sessions pulls relevant concepts from science, counseling and educational psychology, sports medicine, relaxation, human development, and other content areas. The overall goal is to help teens recognize their own stressors and habitual responses to stress, and to develop behaviors that contribute to physical and emotional well-being. While not intending to substitute for therapy or support groups, some of the sessions may build camaraderie and "bonding" that also emerges in group settings.

In "The Whys and Hows of Teaching Teens Lifeskills" (pages 5–24), we provide an overview of the adolescent years *vis-à-vis* stress. We talk about the status of adolescent health in this country and what typical stressors haunt young people. Some guidelines on specific signs of stress are provided. We also explain in greater detail the concepts of stress and how lifeskills are typically acquired. Then we introduce the materials and offer suggestions on how to use them.

In "The Sessions" (pages 25–112), we present twelve complete, self-contained sessions. Each session contains:

- an overview of the session

- a list of the overall goals relevant to the session

- a list of specific learner outcomes

- reference to the relevant chapters in the student book, *Fighting Invisible Tigers: A Stress Management Guide for Teens*

- an agenda of activities

- a list of required and optional resources and materials

- descriptions and ideas for leading activities

- suggestions for other activities and projects

- when applicable, lists of recommended readings and references.

The sessions also contain all of the materials needed, such as leader scripts, participant handouts (which can also be made into overheads), worksheets, guidelines for projects, and inventories. Each participant will also need a copy of the student book, *Fighting Invisible Tigers: A Stress Management Guide for Teens*.

"Supplementary Materials" (pages 113–126) contains additional tools and materials. A short "bibliography" of titles not listed in the reference sections of each session is found on page 127.

....

REFERENCES

1. Moyers, Bill. *Healing and the Mind*. (New York: Doubleday, 1993.)

2. Elkind, David. *All Grown Up and No Place to Go*. (Reading, MA: Addison-Wesley Publishing Co., 1984), p. 161.

3. Warren, Charles W., William A. Harris, and Laura Kann. *Adolescent Health: State of the Nation*. Monograph Series #1: Mortality Trends, Causes of Death, and Related Risk Behavior Among U. S. Adolescents. (Atlanta, GA: U. S. Department of Health and Human Services, Centers for Disease Control and Prevention, 1993), p. 41.

4. *Kids Count Data Book: State Profiles of Child Well-Being*. (Greenwich, CT: Annie E. Cases Foundation and the Center for Social Policy, 1992), p. 19.

5. Ibid., p. 19.

6. Ibid., p. 19.

7. Sprinthall, Norman A., and W. Andrew Collins. *Adolescent Psychology: A Developmental View*, 2nd Ed. (New York: Random House, 1988), p. 398.

8. Elkind, David. Ibid., Chapter 1, especially pages 3–8.

9. *The Next Generation: The Health and Well Being of Young People of Color in the Twin Cities*. (Minneapolis, MN: The Urban Coalition of Minneapolis, 1992), pp. 19, 27.

10. Rode, Pete. *Resiliency and Risk Among Young People of Color*. (Minneapolis, MN: The Urban Coalition of Minneapolis, 1994), pp. 5, 7, 11.

11. Walker, Joyce A., et al. *Outlooks and Insights: Understanding Rural Adolescents*. (Minneapolis, MN: University of Minnesota, Adolescent Health Program, 1990), p. 15.

12. Warren, Charles W., et al. Ibid., p. v.

13. Ibid., p. 41.

14. Ibid., p. 41.

....

THE WHYS AND HOWS OF TEACHING TEENS LIFESKILLS

TEENAGERS UNDER STRESS

"Contemporary American society has struck teenagers a double blow. It has rendered them more vulnerable to stress while at the same time exposing them to new and more powerful stresses than were ever faced by previous generations of adolescents."[1]

—David Elkind, *All Grown Up and No Place To Go*

Stress is part of the human condition. What aspects of stress are most unique to teenagers, or most important for teachers and others to understand as they work with young people? In this section, we first try to get a grasp on the status of adolescent health in America. How stressed are they? Then we turn to some of the developmental tasks that teenagers face, just by virtue of being teenagers. Then we look at some typical teen stressors (what things they say are difficult for them), and some typical teen reactions to stress (what psychologists can observe and intuit from teenagers' behavior that indicates stress).

THE CURRENT STATUS OF ADOLESCENT HEALTH

How are teens doing? Is adolescence a riskier time today than it was twenty or thirty years ago? By many accounts it is, although the wealth of statistical data on the topic is difficult to sort out and it may not be possible to ever get a truly objective perspective on the matter, as we tend to see the worst in our own times and glorify the past "when things were simpler." We've also gotten better at measuring certain kinds of problems over time. But a minor amount of research into the condition of today's youth reveals enough to seriously concern us.

"Health" is not as easy to measure as disease (as researchers have pointed out), and mortality is easier to measure than almost any other condition or problem. So, beginning with mortality rates for teens, what do we find? At first glance, we see that in the past decade the annual rates of death were relatively low: 27 teens (per 100,000) in the 10-to-14-year-old age group, 86 teens (per 100,000) for the 15-to-19-year-olds.[2] In general, death rates rise with age group and are highest among the elderly. The 20-to-24-year-old age bracket, for example, has a higher rate of deaths per 100,000 people than the two younger age groupings cited above. But falling mortality rates have been the norm for all age brackets. In fact, "...because of high risk behaviors engaged in by some adolescents and the hazardous environments they may inhabit, the 10-to-19-year-old age group is the only segment of the U. S. population in which mortality rates have not declined substantially in the past 20 years."[3]

Teen deaths are typically divided into five categories: automobile crashes, homicide, suicide, injury, and all other causes. Most recent figures from the Centers for Disease Control and Prevention (CDCP) relate that while the mortality rates of teenagers have been falling overall since 1979, their 12% decline is due primarily to the increased use of seat belts (which reduced the number of automobile fatalities). Other unintentional injuries (a category which includes house fires and farm accidents) have also declined, probably from improved safety standards and equipment. The two categories which have gone up are suicide (+8%) and homicide (+7%). Looking specifically at the leading cause of death for young people ages 10 to 24 in 1987–88, CDCP found that the primary cause for white males and females was car crashes, followed by "other" deaths, suicide, and unintentional injuries. For black males the leading cause—which accounted for twice as many deaths as any other cause—was homicide.

Table 1				
Leading Causes of Teen Deaths 1987–88				
(Percent of total deaths)				
	Car Crash %	Homicide %	Suicide %	Injury %	Other %
White male	42.0	7.8	15.8	13.9	20.5
White female	42.3	7.5	8.5	7.0	34.8
Black male	17.6	41.3	6.1	11.6	23.4
Black female	15.0	23.9	3.8	8.0	49.4

From: *Adolescent Health: State of the Nation.* Monograph Series #1: Mortality Trends, Causes of Death, and Related Risk Behaviors Among U.S. Adolescents. (Atlanta, GA: U.S. Department of Health and Human Services, Centers for Disease Control and Prevention, 1993), p. 41.

Thus, when one looks closer at mortality figures, one finds an ominous rise in deaths that are related to extreme emotional distress and dysfunctional circumstances. These circumstances are in turn related to poverty, race (and racism), and a host of other factors. Both suicide and homicide are most usually reactions of an individual to psychosocial factors in their lives, not biological organisms. (Some suicides may be related to genetically predisposed depression, however.) While physicians studying the incidence of childhood disease find that physical health is relatively good (asthma, for example, is the biggest single physical problem), "developmental, learning, and behavioral disorders are among the most prevalent chronic conditions of childhood and adolescence."[4]

Some of the more important indicators of teen health concern alcohol and drug use. Teenage drug use has been tracked by many researchers, and most have found that use increased during the 1970s, peaked in the early 1980s, and then began declining. The two most recent annual national surveys by the University of Michigan's Institute for Social Research, however, find that drug use has been on the upswing again, for the second year in a row. Nearly half of all the 50,000 high school seniors surveyed in a representative, random sample report that they had tried illegal drugs. This is an increase of 3.2% from the previous year. Most of the increase is due to increased use of marijuana. While the usage overall is still below the peak years, United States Secretary of Health Donna Shalala feels the trend is ominous and reflects drug glorification messages in our popular culture.[5]

Perhaps even more tenacious than illicit drug use is the very widespread abuse of alcohol, which begins in grade school. The abuse of alcohol especially at the college level is receiving new attention, as non-drinkers and moderate drinkers are beginning to assert themselves in dormitories and campuses across the country.[6] As reported in *Time* magazine, a recent study by the Harvard School of Public Health documented the prevalence of undergraduate drinking by surveying 17,592 students at 140 schools. They found that nearly half of students are "binge" drinkers (defined as consuming four or five drinks at one time, on at least three occasions, in the previous two weeks). Importantly, the study also documented the effect that drinking has, both on the drinkers themselves and on other students. Forty percent or more of all binge drinkers also reported missing classes, forgetting where they were or what they did, engaging in unplanned sex, and having five or more alcohol related problems during the school year (such as getting hurt, damaging property, having unprotected sex, or getting into trouble with campus police). Over half of all the students surveyed reported having to care for drunken students on some occasion, having their study or sleep interrupted, or enduring some other problem, such as insults or humiliations, unwanted sexual advances, arguments, property damage, or assault by a drunken student. Having 50% of the student body essentially *drunk* six times a month suggests that this age group has adopted a harmful, non-productive strategy for escaping the stresses they face.

Abusing drugs and alcohol is not the only risky behavior engaged in by teens, of course. In a large survey study of youth conducted in the late 1980s in 111 communities (mostly in the Midwest) involving over 46,000 students in grades 6–12, some 20 identified risk behaviors were tracked across age groups.[7] These behaviors clustered into nine categories: alcohol, tobacco, illicit drugs, sexuality, depression/suicide, anti-social behavior, school, vehicle safety, and food disorders. Respondents were students living in communities with populations of 100,000 or less, with a predominantly white, middle-class citizenry. In these supposedly more secure, non-urbanized settings in middle America, seniors in high school reported the following:

- 39% had one or more episodes of "binge drinking" (drinking until drunk) in the previous two weeks

- 33% drove a car while drunk at least twice in the previous year

- 46% rode in a car with a drunk driver at least twice in the previous year

- 57% said they never use a seat belt

- 60% were sexually active, and of those who were active, 47% had not used contraceptives

- 15% reported significant depression

- 15% reported attempted suicide.

In this same study, 21% of the total youth surveyed reported feeling "under stress or pressure most or all of the time." The percentage of students responding at this level escalated each year from 6th grade (11%) to 12th grade (27%). In looking at gender differences, these researchers found that by 12th grade, 23% of the girls reported one or more incidents of sexual abuse, and 21% reported one or more incidents of physical abuse. Thirty-four percent—over one-third of all female seniors—had experienced either physical or sexual abuse, or both at some point in their lifetimes. Compared to boys, girls reported higher stress levels and depression, and attempted suicide more often. (Boys are more frequently successful, however, which has led to a higher suicide rate for males.) This profile suggests a significant amount of emotional stress, lack of knowledge about consequences of risky behaviors, lack of knowledge about alternatives to risky behaviors, poor judgment, and inappropriate coping strategies in the face of stress.

Other researchers have looked at the predictors of emotional stress in teens and have separated out the results by race and gender.[8] Emotional stress in one study was measured by analyzing a subset of questions from a large, periodic statewide survey of youth done in Minnesota since the mid-1980s. Three variables were significant predictors of high emotional stress in all five of the ethnic groups studied (African American, American Indian, Asian, Chicano/Latino, and white, in the language of the survey). These variables were: boredom, negative body image, and worries about violence. Other predictors included worries about violence and physical abuse. Simply being female and Asian predicted a certain amount of emotional stress.

When researchers in the same study looked at suicide risk, they found that the Chicano/Latino group had the highest percentage of teens with recent suicidal thoughts and attempts (16.2%) followed by Asian (14.4%) and American Indian youth (14.2%), African American teens (13.5%), and white adolescents (9.3%). The strongest predictors of suicide risk were high emotional stress (most predictive for white students) and recent mental or emotional problems in the family (most predictive for American Indian students).

Compilation of research by Dr. Michael Rutter, a child psychologist in England, indicates that several major disorders increase significantly during adolescence: 1) depression, 2) alcoholism and drug dependency, 3) anorexia nervosa, and 4) attempted suicide.[9] While young children can suffer from depression, and alcoholism and drug abuse and eating disorders can begin before puberty, suicide is virtually unheard of in children. International research finds that about 10–20% of the adolescent population has a significant, generally recognizable psychological "disturbance" at some point. While this is perhaps less than the widespread notion that all teenagers experience a tumultuous passage into adulthood, one out of every five teens makes such "disturbance" a fairly common event.

At one time, teen pregnancy was a very uncommon (although certainly not unheard of) problem. Not so today. Perhaps the most painful of all indicators is that of the pregnancy rate for unmarried teen girls. Nationwide, in 1989, "the number of babies born to single teens was 347,880, or 8.6 percent of all births—a 14% increase in the percent of all births to teens over the decade."[10] Although recent data suggests that the rate has been leveling off for young white women, the rate continues to escalate for young African American women. It is trends such as these that signal a major time bomb for those of us working in the social services or with youth, for unwed mothers are more likely to resort to welfare, more likely to be stuck in a life of poverty. One current estimate reports that one-half of all black children and one-third of all Hispanic children live in poverty.[11]

In answer to the question, "How are teens doing?," we can say that some are managing quite well despite difficult circumstances, and some are even thriving, but for many, life is very tough. Adolescence in America is a hazardous time, even for young people with lots of good things going for them (e.g., family connectedness, structure in their lives, caring adults). To work with teens, and to teach them skills for coping, we need to understand the tigers they have to deal with in their external and internal worlds. For most teens, the internal "developmental" tigers—their own demons—are the greatest challenge. While these tigers are not, by and large, avoidable, they are foreseeable—which means we can help teens prepare for them.

THE DEVELOPMENTAL TASKS OF TEENS

Although more current research challenges the stereotype of adolescence as a universally stress-filled period, the first psychologist in the United States, G. Stanley Hall, characterized the transition from childhood to adulthood as full of *Sturm und Drang*— "stress and storm." Erik Erikson, the well-known developmental psychologist, also saw the period as naturally full of tension. "The eye of the storm is not hormonal—or sexual, or physical—change alone; it is the task of bringing all of these changes together with the uncertain expectations about, and hopes for, the future into a coherent self-concept—an identity."[12] Cognitive psychologists, such as Jean Piaget, were instrumental in theorizing how youth begin to think at a higher level—more abstractly, analytically, critically, and with greater insights and perspective—than they had as children. Together with the physical changes of puberty, the experience of love and romance and sex, and the search for values and meaning in an incoherent and unjust world—all of these processes contribute to the larger gestalt of adolescence.

As someone who works with teens, you probably know the developmental challenges and changes as well as anyone. You know their strong surge for independence, the need to test limits and take risks, the intense feelings that accompany this period of life. Mixed in with the hormonal changes of puberty and the psychological search for identity is the stress of accomplishment and mastery—that is, the need to develop competency in different skill areas and situations. This may be especially important in the United States, where individualism and competition are a way of life. Once in high school, the illusion of equality (i.e., everyone has equal talents, abilities, resources, and options) falls away rather dramatically as students sort themselves (or get sorted) into different ability groups, socioeconomic and racial groups, and other cliques. Part of the normal developmental process, therefore, involves learning how to compete on the playing field, in the classroom, in the social arena. Inevitably, the challenge of growing up includes learning how to lose before a larger and more judgmental public eye. The stakes get higher the older one gets, as well. Winning and losing mean not just who wins the soccer game or gets to date the prom queen, but who gets an after-school job, who gets into college, who gets "the good life" pictured on TV. In America, a lot of importance is attached to winning, to "making it," to being successful as an individual. This complicates the already challenging process of becoming an adult and produces the "James Dean" stereotype of angry, alienated youth. Perhaps it helps to explain why the work of some cultural anthropologists challenges the notion that adolescence has to be rebellious and problem-filled, since in other societies "the transition between childhood and adulthood may be smooth, rather than turbulent."[13]

TYPICAL TEEN STRESSORS

Given the "natural" challenges that come from within, in combination with stresses from the external world, teens worry about a lot of things (see "Teen Inventory on Common Stressors and Stress Symptoms," pages 47–50). Some of the things they worry about change from year to year, as certain fears and questions subside and new ones crop up. Others are more or less constant—they just take on different degrees of importance or qualities.

Sex

High on most teenagers' lists (at any time from 6th to 12th grade) is sex. The 7th or 8th grader will worry most about the physical changes of puberty. Height, weight, the onset of menses, the embarrassment of menstruation, the size of breasts, body hair and body odor, facial features, acne, physical size and strength, unexpected erections, wet dreams, overall attractiveness—the list is long and every item very intense. By high school, the more crucial preoccupation turns to sex itself: When is "it" going to happen? With whom? Under what circumstances? Who else is "doing it"? In some cases, the topic of sex is even more supercharged with anxiety, if homosexuality, sexual harassment, abuse, or incest are part of the picture.

Friends

Teens also worry a lot about their friendships, as Session 7 ("Communication Styles") and Session 9 ("Trusting Relationships") discuss. Relationships take on a whole new meaning in adolescence, and not just between teens who are dating or interested in each other sexually. Friendships help the adolescent define who he or she is. Belonging to a group is a way to establish identity and test out new values. Many of the expectations and needs teens have of one another go unspoken, but they are very real. The support and the heartache that friends provide can be very intense. Teens therefore worry about being liked, about being included in the right crowds. As they take on new risks, they worry about being made fun of, or being rejected. As they explore more serious romantic relationships, they worry about loyalty, commitment, intimacy.

If you have teenagers at home and have ever wondered how on earth they could possibly spend so much time on the telephone, the answer is all about friendships: maintaining, testing, and reforming the social network which makes them feel secure and clear about who they are and where they stand. Of course, talking to friends on the telephone also gives them something to do! This year (in at least one author's household) could be dubbed "The Year of the Beeper and Car Phone." Not content to be out of communication with friends for longer than a millisecond, teenagers have begun using the latest in technology. The purpose of such gadgetry is to check out who is doing what at any given moment, to locate the most interesting gathering, to better compare competing invitations, and to arrange car pools. (Some teens also reportedly call their parents to relay information about their whereabouts.) Whether this non-stop communication is constructive, or merely another elaborate defense against household chores, homework, or learning how to deal with time alone, is yet to be known. What it does speak to is the importance of the peer group, and the underlying anxiety about not fitting in, or not having friends to be with.

School

School is the stage where many of the teenage social roles are played out. It is also, of course, the place where accomplishment and mastery are tested, and a more serious pecking order ensues. Teens worry a lot about success in school, be it in the classroom or in extracurricular activities. When you think about it, competition is an underlying element throughout virtually every school activity. For by high school, only the good players make the team; only the good singers or actors get the parts in the school play; only the popular kids get elected to the student council or other leadership positions. It is a rare teacher who is able to overcome the very strong cultural norms of our society, and the teenagers' own sense of competition, and create a climate of learning that supports the doing of things for their own sake, and the innate pleasure that comes with mastery. Given parental and societal pressure to succeed, it is no surprise that teens worry about exposing themselves to failure. Performance and grades are the bottom lines.

Parents and Leaving Home

Teens also worry about their imminent departure from parents and home—what that means and how to do it. In the earlier teenage years, the anxiety may relate first to being physically separated (e.g., spending the summer away at camp, traveling with another family on vacation, or having extended time at home alone while a parent works). The "all-grown-up 7th grader" suddenly can't eat the "funny food they serve," or can't really sleep without hearing the familiar hall clock tick.

On another level, the anxiety concerns who is in control, which rules are "real" and which are optional, and the whole process of testing expectations and norms: "Will I be caught if I break a rule?" "What will the parent or teacher do if they find out I broke the rule?" This applies to norms of the peer group, as well as authority. Underlying this anxiety are several important questions that relate to the building of a separate identity: "Is the rule fair?" "Do I have a right to not follow the rules?" "If I don't follow the rules, will I be more or less respected (by my peers, by my parents)?" "Whose approval do I really want?" "Will I still be loved if I go against the family tradition, or make choices that are different from the norm?" This, then, leads into the difficult questions of values and choices (moral development) and becoming one's own person.

For teens who have not had good relationships with parents, the anxieties may be complicated by the lack of feeling loved, or the fear of not measuring up to expectations. Depending on the home situation, the anxieties may have more to do with getting parental attention or approval rather than separation. Naturally, if parents themselves have problems (i.e., domestic violence, chemical addiction, employment instability), then teens may have a different host of concerns, including fear for their own safety or concern for the viability of the family. The separation task becomes all that more difficult for teens who have not had some degree of family connectedness and stability. They may look or act more "separate," but they often lack the skills and maturity to take on the adult roles in which they find themselves.

Toward the end of high school, the task of leaving home once again takes on a physical and tangible dimension. It can also take on an air of finality. The tenor of the actual leave-taking can vary tremendously, depending on whether teens are on a fast and abrupt track (i.e., no financial support from parents, and the teens are no longer living at home), or a track that has been mediated by college, or other plans involving some level of family support. The potential stresses for this period of adolescence are then as diverse and numerous as for adulthood. They include the stresses (and consequences) of personal decision-making on everything from selecting a college major to figuring out living arrangements to getting jobs to marriage and having children.

From the Mundane to the Existential

During the bulk of adolescence, however, teens tend to worry about things in their own immediate lives and the near future. They worry about sex, about friends, about the immediate next steps related to separating from parents and becoming their own person. Some of their worries can be exceptionally practical and nitty-gritty, such as:

- simply getting up and getting to school on time
- not losing their notebook or car keys
- completing assignments
- passing exams.

Other anxieties are more far-reaching:

- having enough money to get all the things they want
- keeping up with other young people who have fancier cars, more expensive clothes, greater freedom, more exotic vacations
- avoiding conflict with peers and adults
- adjusting to physical or intellectual handicaps, or chronic illness
- feeling comfortable in a school environment where violence and abuse are commonplace
- getting home safely in an unsafe neighborhood
- changing schools due to a parent's relocation
- dealing with parents who are fighting, alcoholic or drug dependent, or abusive
- dealing with racism or sexism
- coping with major changes in the family, such as birth, death, divorce, remarriage.

Depending on the young person's circumstances, these fears and worries can be small or all-consuming.

Some teens also worry about the society they are growing up in. They may fear for some particular threat to their neighborhood (e.g., increasing crime and violence, a new highway being built, air pollution from a nearby industry). Or they may be angry at the injustice of society generally and worry about poverty, the environment, the dangers of nuclear energy, and global warfare. While much has been made of the apathy of "Generation X" in comparison to reformers in the baby-boom generation, it seems to us that teenagers are still very much capable of the kind of idealism that fueled the youth movement of the 1960s. True, many seem disinterested, hopeless, or concerned only about the things that touch their own lives. (One could say the same of most adults, as well!) The adolescent nature, however, is often quite sensitive to injustice (having recently "discovered" it), and teens can often be drawn in to discussions of social policy and current events. And some will be bothered enough by "man's inhumanity to man" to take action.

TYPICAL TEEN REACTIONS TO STRESS

"Yes, the world has become an exciting place, but in this new world adolescents feel much more exposed and therefore more vulnerable than ever before. Things can get scary, even terrifying, and perhaps overwhelming."[14]

—Anthony E. Wolf, *Get Out of My Life, But First Could You Drive Me and Cheryl to the Mall?*

Often, when adults look at teenagers, we see them having a very good time. When we compare their lives to the lives we led at their age, we may feel we had even more responsibilities and less freedoms, and think they are getting the "better end of the stick." And, indeed, many teens do have lots of fun, much of the time. But some of that fun has a manic, out-of-control aspect to it. Sometimes it is hard to see that beneath the bravado and the high-spirited laughter, there is a lot of tension.

What are the common signs of teen stress? Basically, teens react to stress in ways that are consistent with their personalities. Some face stressors directly, others indirectly. Some are active in their expression of stress, others take a passive route. The actual symptoms they exhibit are really not too different than the symptoms that adults show (see "Teen Inventory on Common Stressors and Stress Symptoms," pages 47–50). In all likelihood, teens' manner of coping mirrors that of parents and other family members. The possible signs of stress include the following:

- general irritability; arguing about everything, however minor

- regressive or immature behavior; they want their own way, they want it now, they can't tolerate change from routine, and they are excessively sensitive to demands, expectations, or what sounds like criticism

- obsession with external appearances and material goods; lots of time spent looking "right," having the right haircut, car, stereo equipment, etc.

- school phobia; avoiding school work, cutting classes; sudden drop in academic performance

- secretiveness; lying about whereabouts or actions

- chronic dissatisfaction; nothing is good enough (including themselves)

- loss of interest or pleasure in things they used to enjoy

- excessive sleeping or sleeplessness

- difficulty concentrating

- significant change in eating habits

- excessive or ongoing worrying

- frequent crying spells

- increase in the number of accidents or mishaps

- frequent colds, flu, or other communicable diseases and chronic conditions

- withdrawal; spending a lot of time alone; saying "no" to invitations from friends

- daydreaming, excessive fantasizing

- hyperactivity

- escapist behaviors (e.g., excessive TV watching).

Gender Differences

In addition to individual personality characteristics, there are some fairly typical gender differences in the way that young men and women respond to stress. Psychologist Anthony Wolf describes the difference from the perspective of parents and family relationships.[15] He reports that boys suddenly become "vanishing experts" around the house. They spend a lot of time away from home with their peers, "hanging around the neighborhood." As in Tennessee Williams' play, *The Glass Menagerie*, they are "Going out, just *out*," and are extremely reluctant to state where, with whom, or when they are likely to return (they usually don't know). In order to avoid messy conflicts with parents, they say "yes" to requests or demands, but then simply avoid fulfilling the request. They leave the premises. Especially with their mothers, boys can become extremely private and rejecting of any maternal behavior that suggests either physical or psychological intimacy. Wolf finds boys to be generally less verbal and more physical in their response to stress than girls. The physical expression can either be active (e.g., throwing things, putting a fist into the wall, slamming a door) or extremely passive (e.g., becoming a "slug" in front of the TV, reading comic books in bed for hours on a Saturday morning).

Wolf notes that in contrast, teenage girls are often more verbal in dealing with stress. At home, they may engage in non-stop verbal sparring with siblings or parents. They also can adopt "sneaky and lying" behaviors, and spend more time manipulating friends and family in an effort to bolster their self-esteem or status. They tend to be more aware of subtle changes in relationships than boys, and more vocal in expressing insecurity, jealousy, and competitiveness. Actually, the description Wolf provides fits a female teenager who is overt in responding to stress; we believe there is a flip side to this, and that is the passive female who holds all her feelings inside and attempts to keep a very controlled image on the surface.

Other researchers, who surveyed students in grades 6 through 12 in a national study of assets, deficits, and risk behaviors, found significant gender differences.[16] These differences are summarized in Table 2 on page 14. Developmental *assets* are those resources that a young person has personally or in his or her environment that provide nurture, guidance, and positive opportunities to grow. *Deficits* are, conversely, the lack of such assets and the presence of potentially negative conditions, influences, and opportunities. Teens' responses to survey items reinforced the general belief that girls turn inward with their stress, while boys "act out." Girls are more conforming, boys are more rebellious.

While the column on the right of the table (which lists the variables for which no gender differences were found) is long, the number of variables which distinguished girls from boys is quite interesting. Although girls reported more of the identified assets than boys, they were also more likely to report physical or sexual abuse, significant stress, depression, and suicide attempts. Boys, despite their *lack* of assets, were more likely to report high self-esteem and decision-making skills. The common male deficits were overexposure to TV and hedonism; their at-risk behaviors were external in orientation (e.g., group fighting, theft and vandalism) rather than internal.

Generalizations can be helpful in that they help us anticipate what the teens we are working with may do or not do, feel or not feel, at any given time. But like any generalization, the gender differences stated here can't predict every case. A person's reaction to stress will be a product of all that they are, inclusive of the environment in which they live, which embraces many factors in addition to gender.

In regards to potential suicide, some predicating factors were outlined by David Elkind.[17] Generally speaking, teens who attempt suicide have a background of depression that is ignited by a particular stressor. While some of the triggers may appear transitory or minor to adults (e.g., the break-up with a boyfriend or girlfriend), they can assume ultimate importance to the teenager. Some of the more well-known triggers include:

- death of a family member
- divorce or separation of parents
- personal or family problems with the law
- personal injury, or chronic illness of self, family member, or friend
- marriage of a sibling; remarriage of a parent
- being fired from a job; a parent's being fired
- retirement of a parent
- drastic change in health of family member or friend
- pregnancy, abortion, or birth of baby.

TABLE 2
GENDER DIFFERENCES IN ASSETS, DEFICITS, AND AT-RISK BEHAVIOR

	GIRLS MORE THAN BOYS*	BOYS MORE THAN GIRLS*	NO GENDER DIFFERENCES
ASSETS	Achievement motivation Other adult communication Time at home Involved in church/synagogue Educational aspirations Care about people's feelings Homework Concern for world hunger Involved in music Parental monitoring Parental standards Positive peer influence Values sexual restraint Values helping people	Decision-making skills Self-esteem	Other adult resources Assertiveness skills Positive school climate Parental discipline Friendship-making skills Parents as social resources Parent communication Parent involvement, school Planning skills Family support Positive view of future School performance Involved in community organizations/clubs Involved in school extracurricular activities
DEFICITS	Physically abused Sexually abused Stress	TV overexposure Hedonism	Negative peer pressure Drinking parties Social isolation Alone at home Parental addiction
AT-RISK BEHAVIOR	Depression Attempted suicide	Seat belt non-use Frequent chewing tobacco use Binge drinking Group fighting Police trouble Sexually active Theft Vandalism	Frequent alcohol use Bulimia Daily cigarette use Non-use of contraceptives Driving and drinking Weapon use Frequent use of illicit drugs Riding and drinking School absenteeism Desire to drop out

* Only gender differences of 5% or more are listed. Reported gender differences are statistically significant, $p < .0001$.

From: Peter Benson. *The Troubled Journey: A Portrait of 6th–12th Grade Youth.* (Minneapolis, MN: Search Institute and the Lutheran Brotherhood, 1993), p. 61.

SUMMARIZING TEEN STRESS

In conclusion, this has been a brief look at adolescent stress. Today's teenagers face very real stressors related to identity formation: Who are they going to be in this world? Think of the decisions that teens have to make at an earlier and earlier age—decisions related to sexuality, drugs, and the standards of the peer group, parental expectations, and their own future. Studies show that teens who survive this transition period have at least one adult they trust and can talk to. Caring adults are those people who can listen and affirm a young person's need to explore and make decisions, and at the same time provide some guidance and support—more by role modeling and gentle questioning than lecturing. We'd like to think that more adults can get into the picture by teaching teens lifeskills.

. . . .

REFERENCES

1. Elkind, David. *All Grown Up and No Place to Go.* (Reading, MA: Addison-Wesley Publishing Co., 1984), p. 6.

2. Warren, Charles W., William A. Harris, and Laura Kann. *Adolescent Health: State of the Nation.* Monograph Series #1: Mortality Trends, Causes of Death, and Related Risk Behavior Among U. S. Adolescents. (Atlanta, GA: U. S. Department of Health and Human Services, Centers for Disease Control and Prevention, 1993), p. 41.

3. *The Future of Children: U. S. Health Care for Children,* vol. 2, no. 2. (Los Angeles: Center for the Future of Children and the David and Lucile Packard Foundation, 1992), p. 9.

4. Ibid., p. 25.

5. "More Teens Using Drugs," as reported by the News Services in the *Minneapolis Star Tribune,* December 13, 1994, pp. 1 and 14A.

6. Gorman, Christine. "Higher Education: Crocked on Campus." *Time* magazine, December 19, 1994, pp. 66–67.

7. Benson, Peter L. *The Troubled Journey: A Portrait of 6th–12th Grade Youth.* (Minneapolis: Search Institute and the Lutheran Brotherhood, 1993), p. 43.

8. Rode, Pete. *Resiliency and Risk Among Young People of Color.* (Minneapolis, MN: The Urban Coalition of Minneapolis, 1994), p. 7.

9. Warren, Charles W., et al. Ibid., p. 385.

10. *Kids Count Data Book: State Profiles of Child Well-Being.* (Greenwich, CT: Annie E. Cases Foundation and the Center for Social Policy, 1992), p. 12.

11. Ibid.

12. Sprinthall, Norman A., and W. Andrew Collins. *Adolescent Psychology: A Developmental View,* 2nd Ed. (New York: Random House, 1988), p. 156.

13. Ibid., p. 12.

14. Wolf, Anthony E. *Get Out of My Life, But First Could You Drive Me and Cheryl to the Mall?* (New York: The Noonday Press, 1991), p. 15.

15. Ibid., pp. 42-49.

16. Benson, Peter L. Ibid., p. 61.

17. Elkind, David. Ibid., p. 188.

. . . .

WHAT ARE LIFESKILLS?

Lifeskills are an assortment of behaviors that can reduce stress and help us maintain physical and psychological health. Examples of lifeskills are found in people who know how to relax and take good care of their physical health. Lifeskills include knowledge about relationships, communication, and expressing feelings. Lifeskills also include learning how to get control over some of life's stressors through assertiveness, time management, goal setting, and planning. Lifeskills are tactics that build rather than drain energy; they fortify people for living, as well as heal their wounds.

The concept of lifeskills is closely tied to the concept of stress. In fact, in this book, we use lifeskills and stress management skills somewhat synonymously. In and of itself, stress is neither all bad nor all good. Certainly, it is an important part of life. Accurately stated, "stress" is a biologically inherited response of humans to any number of potentially threatening triggers or stimuli. When stimulated by either a sudden surprise or shock, a verbal attack, an abstract worry, or an unconscious nightmare, we experience a shot of neurochemicals to the brain. What follows then is a succession of other physical and psychological reactions: increased pulse rates, rapid breathing, fear, and restlessness. This supply of energy can be very positive and useful. If it becomes chronic or long-term, it can also be debilitating and greatly detract from the quality of life.

What people do with particular triggers (stressors) and their own reactions (stress patterns) differs greatly from individual to individual, as seen in the previous sections. To begin with, what seems stressful to one person may not seem stressful to another. What one person's heart would do, were he or she poised on the threshold of an airplane's open door, is different than what an experienced sky diver's would do because of the differences in training, experiences, and temperaments. Even when two equally trained people are faced with the same stressful event, their perceptions (and thus their responses) may be very different.

We believe people can learn to be more skillful in managing stress-producing situations than is commonly believed. Some of us are naturally more successful at it than others. In fact, the cave dwellers who survived in primitive eras were probably those who knew best when and how to fight or flee; they knew how to respond most appropriately to stress, and therefore, lived to produce another generation. Today's successful adults are (similarly) those people who learn how to respond to stress appropriately in self-nurturing, creative, and assertive ways. Instruction in lifeskills, therefore, doesn't simply call for superior coping strategies (i.e., better "pain relievers," although they do have their place), but for more resourceful stress management skills.

A CONTINUUM OF LIFESKILLS DEVELOPMENT

People vary tremendously in regards to their awareness of stress. Some appear to be oblivious to it; others are quite sensitive. Most typically, awareness of stress grows out of an experience of physical pain or limitation. A visit to the doctor reveals that mid-morning headaches—the ones that begin behind the left eye and travel with exquisite pain to the right—are stress-related. Or people begin to read and question on their own why they have gastric ulcers, need to chain-smoke, or suffer from teeth clenching, backaches, stiff necks, frequent crying, sleepless nights, lethargy, or compulsive eating.

People with chronic stress usually begin to recognize a cycle, a pattern, in terms of what factors or events precede their symptoms, or contribute to their condition. They may then decide to move to the offensive by experimenting with various remedies or "programs": Weight Watchers, aerobics, Al-Anon, jogging, group therapy, Outward Bound, Nautilus. If they find something that "works" for them—and it may be routine physical activity, more sleep, less alcohol, a better diet, relaxation, daily talks with a friend, less work, more stimulating work, a different work pattern, some combination of the above, or some activity or routine altogether different—they may find themselves swearing by that method(s) because it keeps them going and makes life better. We call whatever it is they are doing a lifeskill.

The figure below summarizes the stages of lifeskills development. The continuum runs from "Unaware of Stress" to "Incorporating Lifeskills to Enhance Life." On this continuum, one sees the development of increased awareness of stress, and increased skill in stress management.

At the farthest point at one end of the continuum ("Unaware of Stress") we find people who are generally unaware of stress. They don't really know what they are feeling, or even what makes them feel "bad" or "good." They may be in a chronic state of lethargy or apathy. It is possible that they simply don't have any stress in their lives. What's more likely is that they are in some state of denial. They've adopted the attitude that it is bad to express feelings, pain, or negative thoughts. They may feel ashamed of such feelings, and disregard the subject of stress management as being for "sissies." Teens in this stage may have adopted the stance that "Nothin' bothers me." "Hey—I'm cool." They may also be intolerant of other people who are willing to talk about life's challenges. "What is she whining about?" Another explanation for the apparent lack of awareness of stress is that it has been so omnipresent in their lives, teens just don't really know what it means to feel

alert but really relaxed (as opposed to asleep or stoned). For that reason, we spend time in the early sessions simply getting teens to differentiate between a state of tension and a state of deep relaxation.

At the next point or stage of lifeskills development, "Intellectually Aware of Stress," the biological facts of stress are learned and accepted as true—but in an abstract way. "Yes, stress is something that is out there and affects all humans." But people in this stage haven't yet really analyzed their own stressors or stress reactions. They can recognize the symptoms of stress in other people; they can differentiate between "good" and "bad" stress, between positive and negative coping strategies. And they are likely to agree that the subject of stress is important—but it may not yet have a whole lot of personal relevance to them. "Yeah, stress is bad—but it happens to others; can't happen to me." While this stage of awareness may be adequate for some teens for right now, sooner or later (we can predict this with 100% accuracy!) life will sneak up on them and give them a bite. Teaching lifeskills, even to young people who don't think they need them, is important, because it provides them with some knowledge that they will one day need.

At the next point or stage of lifeskills development, "Personally Aware of Stress," teens can say, "Yes, I understand what stress is, and I see it in me." They have internalized the information learned at the previous point or stage and can describe their personal pattern or cycle of stress in some detail. Sources of stress can be named and "overloads" predicted with some accuracy ("I know if I have this third cup of coffee I'll have the biggest headache around 4:00 p.m., but I just can't stop myself"). At this stage, people have learned enough about their own bodies, minds, and habits to know their levels of tolerance for long work hours (for example), or for "hassles," junk food, late-night parties, or family conflicts. These individuals also can identify some of the ineffective ways they've used to block stress in the past (e.g., procrastination, escapism). Several sessions

The Lifeskills Development Continuum

1	2	3	4	5
Unaware of Stress	Intellectually Aware of Stress	Personally Aware of Stress	Building Lifeskills to Manage Stress	Incorporating Lifeskills to Enhance Life

in this guide help teens identify their stressors and know when they've reached their limits of coping and need help.

At the next point or stage of lifeskills development, "Building Lifeskills to Manage Stress," individuals shift from passively reacting to stressors to asserting some controls over them. When possible, they now choose to moderate or eliminate sources of negative stress within their environment, and to search out alternative behaviors that give back a sense of strength, energy, or peace. Although not all of the attempts made at this stage will be well thought-out, consistent, or "successful," they represent concerted effort. More consistently than before, people at stage 4 are learning to reject the "false gods"—the chemicals, the quick-fix habits, the anesthetics, the compulsive behaviors (and we all have them, from workaholism to alcoholism)—and are less willing to be seduced by immediate relief. The attitude of a person at stage 4 is, "I am not helpless; I'm going to get in training and prepare to fight." Although the eight sessions of lifeskills presented here barely touch the surface on skills such as relaxation and assertive communication, they provide an introduction to strategies that many people in cultures around the world have developed over centuries of time.

At the final point on the other end of the continuum, "Incorporating Lifeskills to Enhance Life," we actually do for ourselves that which we know is good. People at this stage have explored and continue to expand on their repertoire of lifeskills, but they do some things routinely to maintain peace and well-being, no matter what their surroundings. They have figured out what they need to do in order to stay reasonably healthy, vital, and "together." They apply this self-knowledge with enough consistency to feel its benefits. And because life is never stagnant, people at this stage continue to branch out and experiment with variations of their lifeskills as they grow older or their situations change. They think proactively of keeping their resources high; they are prepared for unknown "tigers." They believe, "I can be healthy." This is an attitude, a philosophy, which we hope all of the sessions in this guide convey.

HOW ARE LIFESKILLS TYPICALLY LEARNED?

As the above continuum and examples indicate, it takes a long time to develop lifeskills and it's not easy. Most of us have to work at it and continue to refine our strategies throughout our lives. Although lifeskills are probably acquired somewhat sequentially and correlate with age and maturity, the process remains reiterative; we often cycle back to work through earlier stages in order to move forward.

Most of us do not learn lifeskills in school or by thinking about the whole matter hypothetically, however. We learn through experience. It's likely by way of traumatic experience that we face our stressors and the limitations of our preferred coping strategies. For example, some of us learn to slow down and relax as a result of a serious accident or illness. Others learn through divorce the importance of relationships, intimacy, or assertiveness skills. We can learn from depression the benefits of "getting out," visiting friends, volunteer work, or a special hobby. Some of us can learn vicariously from a friend or relative's "bad" experience—a parent's addiction, a coworker's anorexia. Certainly many of us learn key lifeskills by watching healthy people engage in life successfully. But a question worth asking is, why do we learn so late? Some possible reasons include the following:

1. No one teaches us the facts about stress.

Few of us learn anything from others about stress— that a certain amount of stress or stimulation is normal and good; that it's okay to pay attention to the clues your body gives you; that you can gain some control over the amount and type of stress you face. Schools often aren't able or willing to teach students the physical or psychological facts of stress. Although academic, social, and other performance expectations escalate yearly for students as they progress through the system, few teachers or parents counsel them on handling the pressure this creates before a crisis occurs.

2. Many "unwritten" societal norms create stress.

Many cultural norms in our society do not support a moderate lifestyle or pace of life. These norms say, "Be first." "Winning is everything." "Don't be lazy." "Get ahead and make something of yourself." "Don't show your pain." It's common for television ads to tell teenagers, "Go to the limits." "Be wild and crazy." "Make it big." Meanwhile, parents and teachers are saying, "Work up to your potential."

Sociologists studying leisure time habits in this country find that lots of people don't really know what it means to relax. Despite unprecedented affluence, Americans "labor to find the time for leisure pursuits."[1] According to the *Wall Street Journal*, only the Japanese are considered less able to relax, more competitive during "off-hours," and more likely to superimpose business onto leisure time activities than contemporary American business men and women.

We also have a "quick fix" mentality in America in regards to health, in which we expect professionals and medical technology to cure us with a pill or procedure, while we remain essentially passive. Bill Moyers discovered a profound contrast in philosophy in his travels in China and discussions with traditional Chinese doctors for the public television series, *Healing and the Mind*. In traditional Chinese culture, sages taught that "treating someone who is already ill is like beginning to dig a well after you have become thirsty. The classical Chinese physician received a fee only as long as the patient remained in good health. Payments stopped when sickness began. The task was to teach patients to stay healthy by living correctly; temperament, diet, thoughts, emotions, and exercise were all important in a system in which the patient took primary responsibility for sickness or health."[2]

3. We lack cultural norms and role models for managing stress proactively.

In addition to the societal beliefs that actually create stress, we lack the cultural norms and role models for managing stress proactively. Grandparents don't lead their children and grandchildren to the public park every morning, along with all the neighbors, to practice *t'ai chi ch'uan* ("Tai Chi") for 90 minutes, to accomplish what we would call mental and physical

relaxation (stress management). While some critics have come to see the great support group movement in recent years as contributing to a "culture of complaint," we still have taboos against expressing feelings appropriately and seeking support before a major problem (e.g., alcoholism, bulimia, divorce) occurs. We don't usually take the time to educate ourselves about the skills needed to handle stressful life events. Instead, we deny how stressed these events make us feel. We interpret stress as personal weakness, suffer in silence, or declare war on whatever (or whomever) seems responsible for our discomfort.

4. Few adults talk to young people about stress.

Our culture doesn't really know how to encourage children and young adults to develop long-term, healthy behaviors in honest ways. We may lecture on the morality of not smoking or drinking and try to enforce strict rules, but meanwhile, we continue to smoke or drink ourselves, or do nothing about the media which glamorize a smorgasbord of inappropriate behaviors, from promiscuity to drinking and driving and violence. Adult communication that works includes a lot of listening to a young person's experiences and perceptions of stress, then problem-solving with him or her to find better ways to manage stress. A teen is quick to hear, "You shouldn't feel that way," rather than "I understand that you've had it up to here. Would you like to talk about it?" Highly judgmental reactions to an ill-chosen coping strategy deny the reality of the young person's struggle with life and anxiety. Adults lose additional ground when we lecture young people on so-called healthy habits but fail to demonstrate those behaviors ourselves. A perfectionist, depressed, hopeless, angry, or workaholic parent or teacher doesn't offer the troubled teenager a very hopeful picture of adulthood, or many reasons for wanting to grow up.

Results of Typical Lifeskills Learning

As a result of the four reasons described above, children and teens learn to "shut up and live with it" the way the adults in their lives "live with it." Most of us fall into massive, unconscious adaptation to constant stress. For many people, that means accepting and adjusting to their own discomfort and loneliness. After a while, the stooped back feels okay; it only hurts to straighten it. And the "high" that was good enough yesterday is not high enough for today.

SUMMARIZING LIFESKILLS

In summary, inappropriate response to stress contributes to risky behaviors in adolescence. When stress leads to suppression of feelings or chronic depression, it can lead to a diminished immune system and result in physical illness.[3] More immediately, stress depletes energy, impairs functioning, and leads to a stunted life—one without much joy. Many of the inappropriate or ineffective responses to stress begin in childhood, only to come full bloom in adolescence or adulthood. As the statistics in the early part of this chapter illustrate, what teenagers don't know about stress, and their own resources for moderating stress, can be very serious business.

What this adds up to is a rationale for teaching teens a set of lifeskills. Many of us learn too late about stress by experiencing its powerfully negative side effects. Unquestionably, some adolescents will profit by the mistakes of others and the examples of healthy role models, but the learning of lifeskills should not be left to unconscious modeling, or to trial-and-error. It does take time and maturity to shape healthy behaviors, but this process should, logically, be accompanied with direct instruction, discussion, and support.

....

REFERENCES

1. "Working at Relaxation." Special Report: The Business of Leisure. *Wall Street Journal,* Monday, April 21, 1986, p. 1.

2. Moyers, Bill. *Healing and the Mind.* (New York: Doubleday, 1993), p. 253.

3. Ibid., pp. 195–211.

....

ABOUT THIS GUIDE

In the first edition of this guide, published in 1987, these materials were formatted as a twelve-week course (one session per week). Although we knew that not many users were likely to teach all twelve sessions in sequence, we packaged it that way and designed each session in relationship to overarching course goals, keeping in mind the objectives of other sessions. We called it a "teacher's guide" and assumed all participants were students.

While these revised materials are still based on overall goals, and much of the continuity between sessions has been maintained, we recognize that most users will be picking and choosing among sessions and strategies, and fitting in pieces of sessions along with other curriculum materials, ideas, and goals. We have, therefore, downplayed the school-like aspect of the materials and tried to make the sessions a bit more independent of one another. We have eliminated homework assignments and the assumption that projects will be carried over from one session to another. Project ideas are still offered, but without the expectation that subsequent sessions will follow up on them. All in all, we believe these and other changes make the materials more flexible and realistic, given the settings in which they are being used.

THE GOALS OF TEACHING TEENS LIFESKILLS

The overall purpose of these materials is to raise teenagers' awareness of lifeskills. This means beginning with teens at whatever level of awareness they're at on the lifeskills development continuum on page 17 (e.g., completely denying stresses? beginning to differentiate between stressors? understanding the difference between coping and management? open to some new strategies?) and bringing them up to a higher level. This should be considered an introductory level course—a "Whitman sampler of chocolates"—in which four sessions deal with stress, and eight deal with lifeskills (approximately two sessions per lifeskill). With such a brief introduction to lifelong disciplines such as relaxation and aerobics, teens are not expected to become masters at any one lifeskill, unless you spend a lot more time on these areas. It would also be unrealistic to expect teens to progress from the lowest level of awareness of lifeskills to the highest after only twelve sessions. Although the benefits of relaxation or communication skills are great, and tempt us to state lofty goals and promise terrific results, realistically we know it takes a long time to refine and incorporate these skills into our everyday lives.

This overall purpose of increasing teens' awareness of lifeskills translates into five specific goals. Each goal reflects a particular point or stage of lifeskills development on the continuum. Along with the student text, *Fighting Invisible Tigers: A Stress Management Guide for Teens,* these five goals provide the framework around which the sessions were developed.

After completing all twelve sessions, participants should:

1. Know the difference between a state of stress and relaxed well-being.

2. Understand the origins and nature of stress and its effects on health and well-being.

3. Be able to evaluate current stressors, stress levels, and methods of coping.

4. Experience the benefits of a range of lifeskills: physical activity, relaxation, assertiveness, supportive relationships, life planning, and positive "self-talk."

5. Feel empowered to care for themselves and seek help and support when needed.

At the beginning of each session, the overall goal or goals that are particularly relevant for the session are listed. Learner outcomes are also identified.

THE CONTENT OF THE SESSIONS

In revising the session contents, we revisited the six lifeskill areas discussed in *Fighting Invisible Tigers: A Stress Management Guide for Teens.* These areas are: 1) physical activity, 2) relaxation, 3) assertiveness, 4) supportive relationships, 5) life planning, and 6) positive "self-talk" (i.e., as related to perfectionism, risk-taking, and humor). While other lifeskills are possible to teach, we continue to focus on these because they seem to have the broadest application and are not typically addressed in the school curriculum. Theoretically, however, a whole host of strategies could be called "lifeskills," because what makes a particular activity life-enhancing or stress-reducing depends on the individual who uses it.

Each of these areas has been developed into one or more 50-minute sessions and/or woven into the fabric of suggested teaching strategies. The sessions have been designed so that each focuses on a few developmental stages.

THE LEARNING ACTIVITIES

Most sessions begin with some presentation of content by the leader that leads into small group exercises or discussion. Many of the learning activities engage teens either in a role-play or direct experience (e.g., relaxation, aerobic exercises). The learning activities suggested for the earlier sessions require little or no self-disclosure; they are "low risk" for the participant (and leader!). As the sessions progress and group members (presumably) become more familiar with and trusting of each other, the activities start to require more interpersonal sharing. None of the activities are confrontational, however, and teens should always maintain the right not to participate.

Before beginning any of the small group discussion sessions, leaders should repeat the general "rules" of group process:

- No putting anyone down.

- What is shared in the group stays in the group (confidentiality).

- Everyone who wants to participate has the opportunity to participate.

- Everyone shows general courtesy and respect to everyone else.

Most discussions and activities are suitable for groups of between five and twenty-five participants.

WHO SHOULD PARTICIPATE? WHO SHOULD LEAD?

As stated earlier, these materials were originally designed as a course for adolescents in a regular school setting. Our hope is that most, if not all, of the sessions will be incorporated into a quarter or semester course taught by a counselor or health, social studies, or science teacher. The materials may also be appropriate for church groups, 4-H, YMCA, or other community education agencies. Teens in chemical dependency programs, "aftercare" treatment, or other therapy or support groups also could benefit from lifeskills development. Although the materials were written with "prevention" (that is, proactive management of stress) in mind, the basic concepts and strategies certainly apply to young people who have reached a crisis and need a "cure" (that is, more effective lifeskills). A new session was added to complement a new section in the student book, "Self-Care for Tiger Bites." In general, this revision has tried to prepare the leader to be better able to identify teens in crisis, and be prepared to help find appropriate referral services.

As with any interdisciplinary course, it may not be immediately clear who should or could teach this material. Do these sessions belong in science, health, or psychology? Do all teens need them, or only those who are seeing a counselor after school? Do the sessions belong in a homeroom, gifted education, or special education class? Could a concerned health teacher with a desire to do more than sex education and drug awareness lead the sessions?

Depending on what type of school you have, the materials can work in any of these settings, and they can be taught by any of the educators found there. They can also be team taught if one teacher is responsible for coordinating all the sessions. This main teacher is responsible for bringing in the co-teachers or "guest" faculty, for explaining the purpose and philosophy of the materials, and for conducting evaluations. Guest faculty are enlisted to contribute their areas of expertise, such as group dynamics, health, career or goal planning, or assertiveness training. Expert personnel to draw upon include the school nurse, psychologist, science teacher, college counselor, and physical education teacher.

More important than any particular content expertise is the leader's overall interest in stress management and his or her interpersonal style with students. The primary adult leader should have good group process (facilitator) skills and feel comfortable with a degree of personal disclosure. She or he should be able to set the tone for the sessions and be an appropriate role model (e.g., accept diversity of behaviors and opinions, be willing to learn new skills). Not a lot of specialized knowledge is necessary; the intellectual concepts of stress and relaxation are not difficult to grasp. Successful teaching of the concepts does require that leaders value the skills and believe in their importance to teens.

When teaching any course for the first time, it's helpful to begin with an idea of how knowledgeable or skillful your participants already are in the content area you're discussing. For this reason, you may want to find out at the beginning of the course:

- How aware of stress (on the average) are these young people?

- Can they describe common stressors, name sources of stress, differentiate between "good" and "bad" stressors, and between manageable and intolerable amounts of stress?

- How advanced are their lifeskills? Can they identify and apply various life-enhancing or support strategies? Are they learning from the strategies

that backfired? Are they exercising some control over the amount or type of stress they face?

You'll want to get a feel for where your participants are at on the continuum of lifeskills development. Chances are, they'll be somewhat aware of different stressors, but only beginning to identify personal stress patterns. They may be able to say, "Life is tough," or "I feel weirded out," even "I feel stressed out." But few students will have enough personal insight to understand the ways in which they contribute to these habitual stress reactions and patterns. For the most part, they (like many adults) blame others for their misery rather than take responsibility for their situation. They are unconsciously adopting the coping mechanisms sanctioned by their peer group (or those exhibited/enforced by parents). In terms of our continuum of lifeskills development, this puts the majority of teens at the middle to low end.

PREPARING TO LEAD THE SESSIONS

We recommend the following preparation for leading this series of sessions.

1. Read *Fighting Invisible Tigers: A Stress Management Guide for Teens.*

2. Review additional readings on relaxation, physical exercise, and communication skills, particularly if you are not already teaching these subjects or well-versed in them. This book does not supply you with "scripts" of every discussion you need to lead on these topics, and you should feel comfortable elaborating on the major concepts. References are supplied in each session, and a short bibliography is found on page 127. But don't hesitate to check out the school library or tap your own private collection.

3. Line up your support team. Talk about the materials, discuss the suitability of the suggested activities, and plan your time. If you have time, find one group of students (one class or special grouping) on which to pilot the materials.

4. Practice the relaxation exercises ahead of time. By rehearsing with people, you'll learn how to modulate your voice, time your cues, and respond

to the crowd's fidgeting or whispering. Any group new to relaxation will invariably have some students who find this activity scary or embarrassing. Be prepared for this and a wide assortment of other reactions as well, such as yawning, falling asleep, and uncontrolled giggling. Practice will help you to sustain the mood and continue on in a relaxed manner. Similarly, if you're unfamiliar with aerobics, practice the exercise suggested on page 68 ahead of time with friends, students, or other teachers. This will help prepare you for the range of physical abilities you'll likely find in the class.

To help you refine the materials and instruction over time, we suggest that you use the "Evaluation Form: Getting Feedback from Participants on the Sessions" on pages 124–125 after each experience of leading these sessions.

THE SESSIONS

PART I

LIFE IN
THE JUNGLE

SESSION 1

RECOGNIZING THE BEAST

Overview

Sometimes it is hard to recognize things we live with every day, simply because they are so omnipresent and we have become so accustomed to them. Stress is one such condition. It exists not only in the lives of human beings, but in the environments of plants and animals. Even the non-living things on earth, like machines, are subject to stress in their service to humans and exposure to the elements. Automobile engineers know this: they design specific tests to better understand the performance of their machines under "normal" and "excessive" stress conditions. To begin a process of building lifeskills, we begin by asking: What does stress look like? What does it feel like in comparison to real relaxation?

In this session, the "faces of stress" are presented and discussed, and the physical distinction between stress and relaxation is experienced in a progressive relaxation exercise. Additionally, the term "lifeskills" is introduced and their connection to stress established.

Overall Goal Relevant to This Session

After completing this session, participants should:

Know the difference between a state of stress and relaxed well-being.

Learner Outcomes

The purpose of this session is to help teens to:

1. Appreciate the wear and tear that stress inflicts on living things.

2. Compare the feelings of deep relaxation with those of stress.

3. Explain the rationale for learning lifeskills.

Relevant Chapters in the Student Book

■ Introduction (pp. 1–7)

■ Part I, "Fighting Invisible Tigers" (pp. 11–19), especially the sections on short- and long-term stress (pp. 14–19)

Agenda

In order to accomplish these outcomes, leaders need to:

1. Present examples on how stress causes wear and tear in humans, plants, and animals (10 minutes).

2. Describe lifeskills, why we need them, and the prerequisites for learning them (15 minutes).

3. Devise a stressful stimulus, followed by a progressive relaxation exercise (25 minutes).

Resources and Materials

■ "Progressive Relaxation Script #1" (pages 32–33) or "Progressive Relaxation Script #2" (pages 33–34)

■ Pictures of stressed animals, plants, machinery, people

■ Chalkboard or easel pad

■ Carpeted classroom or floor mats (optional)

- Handout of "Relaxation Audiotape Project" (page 121) (optional)
- Handout of "Teen Inventory on Relaxation" (page 35) (optional)

Activities

1. Present examples on how stress causes wear and tear on humans, plants, and animals.

Probably every teen in your session already has some awareness of the concept of stress, as the topic has been dealt with pretty extensively in the media. Nonetheless, "stress" can have an abstract quality to it. Because much of today's stress is psychological in origin, rather than physical (that is, we are tense about relationships or performance, rather than dangerous animals), it can seem kind of elusive. To make the effects of stress more palpable or real, begin the session by telling stories or anecdotes in which stress has left a physical, concrete mark. Better yet, see if you can find some photographs of plants, animals, or machinery, that show how these things deteriorated after some stressful events (e.g., severe weather, illness, aging). Photos from a science or psychology textbook, for example, of chimpanzees involved with deprivation research might exemplify the impact of separation anxiety or other negative interventions. (Research on animal behavior, of course, has served as a foundation for much of our knowledge about human behavior related to stress.)

In the event that you can't find any photographs, the following story may serve to illustrate the physical effects of stress on a well-known, common household feature: a pet cat.

"Kitty" was a healthy four-year-old cat who had lived in the Schmitz household since she was six weeks old. When we first brought her home, our (then) nine-year-old dachshund, Rosie, was more or less queen of the house. Nonetheless, Rosie accepted Kitty very well. She even shared her pillow at night with her. We used to smile, seeing the gentle old dog and trusting little cat asleep side by side, heads and tails overlapping.

In fall of 1994, Rosie died. Although we had not intended to get another dog, we were unexpectedly presented with the opportunity to take home a free puppy: a beautiful black Labrador and German shepherd mix. Well, we couldn't resist. From the moment our new dog, Snoop, entered the house, however, Kitty became extremely nervous. After a few tense "fights," in which Kitty hissed and swiped her (declawed) paws in the dog's face, she made herself scarce. She did not eat for several days. She hid under furniture and refused to venture downstairs, after we divided up the territory and began confining the dog to the kitchen. Although she had never done this before, Kitty began urinating on the kitchen bath mat and any clothes left on the floor. And she continued to ignore her food. When we took Kitty to the vet three weeks later, she had lost two and one-half pounds—over 25% of her body weight. When we petted her, you could feel the body ridges of her spine.

The problem, of course, was the presence of a new dog in her environment, possibly compounded by the loss of her old friend, Rosie. The vet said, "She is suffering from stress." Her prescription was for us to spend more time with Kitty, making sure we kept things to her familiar routine. We could try holding her and talking gently to her in the dog's presence. Kitty's health would not return, we were told, until we found ways to relieve her anxiety.

Ask participants if they have had similar pet experiences, or other examples in which they recognized the tangible effects of stress. The point to underscore is: What is the "face" of stress? What does stress "look like?" How does it change people's physical appearance or behavior?

2. Describe lifeskills.

Segue next to the point that stress is part of life. As we will learn more in later sessions, stress is inevitable and can be both "good" and "bad." What we need to do, however, is prepare ourselves to deal with stress. It's as though we were in training; we need to prepare ourselves physically and mentally for unforeseen, as well as foreseeable, stressors. We can do that with lifeskills. Lifeskills are an assortment of life-enhancing, stress-reducing behaviors that can be learned in order to maintain physical and psychological balance. Lifeskills are practical skills that do more than relieve tension: they build self-knowledge and affirm life. These skills are not frequently taught directly in school or other organized group settings.

Rather, most people learn them through life experience, by trial-and-error, and by assembling strategies from different sources.

Review for yourself the "Introduction" (pages 1–3) and "The Whys and Hows of Teaching Teens Lifeskills" (pages 5–20). When defining lifeskills for students, explain that these skills theoretically include any habitual action that:

■ reduces stress over the long-term

■ gives a person more control over stress-creating experiences

■ "gives back" strength, energy, peace; enhances life

■ promotes a sense of wholeness, of healthy psychological and physiological balance.

Give some broad examples of lifeskills, then explain that in these sessions you'll be concentrating on just six major areas:

1. relaxation
2. physical activity
3. communication styles
4. supportive relationships
5. life-planning skills
6. positive "self-talk."

Explain that other lifeskill categories are possible, such as spirituality, self-defense, aesthetic activity (art, dance, music), or eating healthy foods. Young people should feel free to consider what other lifeskill areas are important for them. Ask if anyone can provide an example of another lifeskill area, perhaps one that they currently use.

In order to learn stress management skills, people need to have four things: a supportive environment, some structured learning, practice, and self-acceptance. You're there to provide the supportive environment and structured learning. You want to encourage students to be patient with themselves, and accept where they are with stress and lifeskills. Explain that it does take time to change one's lifestyle habits. Some of the skills applied here in class may feel awkward at first, but with time and patience their benefits will become impressively clear. Nothing you'll be doing is intended to be "scary," but

it may feel awkward and at times difficult. Some of it is going to be new for you, as well, but you're excited about the opportunity to learn with them.

3. Simulate a brief, very stressful experience.

Lead into the main exercise of the day by explaining that often we're unaware of the load of stress we're carrying around. We get so used to this load it actually feels "normal"...normal to be constantly fatigued, or hyper, or sick. We accept and accustom ourselves to a high undercurrent of tension. It then takes something really unusual (CLAP!!) to wake us up.

The word CLAP above is your signal to actually clap your hands and yell as loudly and dramatically as possible. If you aren't good at clapping, slap a ruler hard on the desk, slam a door or desktop, or pop a giant balloon. A siren might be useful, if it doesn't disturb others. The point is to induce the fight-or-flight response in students—to startle them unexpectedly. Whatever stimulus is devised, it must be long enough in duration for the reactions to set in.

As the participants then begin to recover from the "shock," ask them to describe the physical sensations they just experienced. Get them to verbalize the symptoms such as "stomach dropped," "eyes blinked," "held my breath," and write these on the board or easel pad. Tell them that these reactions are part of the fight-or-flight response, and can be contrasted with its opposite—deep relaxation. States of relaxation are to be distinguished between being asleep or unconscious.

4. Conduct a progressive relaxation exercise.

Progressive relaxation techniques focus a person's attention on such things as breathing slowly and deeply, or releasing a series of muscles in a systematic fashion. They were first developed formally (in Western society) by Dr. Edmund Jacobson, a physician who studied muscular tension in the early 1920s.[1] His studies led to progressive relaxation techniques that have been adopted and developed for a range of medical needs including physical therapy, psychotherapy, and childbirth.

To begin this exercise, have the young people lie down on the floor (if possible). If there are no mats and the room is uncarpeted, participants should separate their chairs and relax as best they can in their seats. You will need to modify the relaxation script if this is the case. Two examples of relaxation scripts are included on pages 32–34. You should practice them in advance and time them so you know how to use them.

When conducting the progressive relaxation exercise, remember to keep your speaking rhythm very slow, and pause for several long seconds after commas and periods. The best way to perfect this timing is to rehearse with someone who actually practices the relaxation exercise as you speak. The pauses should get even longer toward the middle of the exercise, when the participants are at their most relaxed point. When it's time to bring them back to the present, quicken your speaking pace. Make your voice stronger and louder, as though to reinforce the message that it's time to return.

Each script can be literally read, but the exact words don't need to be memorized. It's more important that you understand the flow of each exercise. The exercises may be more effective if you tailor the script or put it in your own words. In the first script (pages 32–33), you're essentially inviting teens to relax each part of their bodies one step at a time. To do this, you begin at the feet and move upwards, and have them visualize particular muscle groups or body sections one at a time, then together. We've highlighted the more common areas of the body that hold tension, but you may substitute others (your own!) or invite students to concentrate specifically on any "trouble spots" that resist letting go. In the second script (pages 33–34), after bringing participants to a state of relaxation, you have them systematically tighten, then release different muscle groupings, such as the hands and face.

The phrasing in both scripts may sound repetitious. This is intentional, as repetition helps the relaxation process. When someone is trying to relax, to give in to the experience and "let go," this repetition is necessary and comforting. Don't be afraid to repeat things several times; also don't be afraid to let silence prevail. And finally, don't underestimate the value of suggesting to students that they end the exercise with a smile. Encourage this by smiling yourself, and looking directly at them.

At the end of the relaxation exercise, talk with the participants about their experience. What did it feel like? Did they enjoy it? Was it different than what they expected, or feel like "normally?"

Suggestions for Other Activities and Projects

- Other ideas for creating a brief but stressful experience include the following:

  - Announce that a test that had been scheduled for later in the week will have to be given today, due to the fact that you have been called away for jury duty.

  - Announce that a photographer is coming to take individual photos (close-ups) for a news article on the group (or the school, youth organization, etc.).

  - Tell the group that they have five minutes to write an essay on the value of good health (or some other fairly easy topic relevant to the context for the class) to win a limousine ride to the upcoming homecoming dance or other special event.

- Any number of relaxation or visualization exercises could be substituted for the ones provided here. You may want to write your own script, or purchase a commercial tape. (Try your local college campus bookstore, or other vendors specializing in health or psychology materials.) These exercises can be repeated many times with subtle variations, and used in shorter or longer time periods.

- Given your setting, you may want to expand some of the ideas presented in this session into a project taking several sessions or weeks. One ideal project for youth groups is the making of their own relaxation audiotape. See "Relaxation Audiotape Project" (page 121) for a handout explaining this project.

- An additional assignment that can be used as a preliminary activity or follow-up to this session is "Teen Inventory on Relaxation" on page 35.

- *Healing and the Mind* by Bill Moyers (see "Recommended Reading" below) is a companion to the five-hour public television series of the same name. Produced by David Grubin, the series is available on videotape. Check your local video rental store or public library, or write or call: KCET Video Finders, 4401 Sunset Blvd.,

Los Angeles, CA 90027; (800) 343-4727. Many chapters and conversations in the book concern the therapeutic value of progressive relaxation. The entire Moyers series would be extremely relevant to these materials.

Recommended Reading

■ Moyers, Bill. *Healing and the Mind.* (New York: Doubleday, 1993.)

REFERENCE

1. Samuels, M., and N. Samuels. *Seeing with the Mind's Eye.* (New York: Random House and the Bookworks, 1975), p. 106.

PROGRESSIVE RELAXATION SCRIPT #1

Lie on your back with your eyes closed, your hands at your sides with the palms facing up. Begin to let go of all the control you exert over your body; allow the feeling of relaxation to take over. Slow down your breathing, make it rhythmic. If you can, keep your mouth closed and feel the breath pull in and release through your nose only. As the breath fills your lungs, your abdomen should rise.

You're going to progressively relax each part of your entire body. Take a long, deep breath, then slowly release it. As you let the breath out, let go of all the tension inside you. Allow your whole body to relax. Now, begin thinking specifically of your feet. Send a visual message to your feet. Tell them to release any feeling of tightness. Make them loose and soft. Next, release any tension in your calf muscles and around your knees. They feel calm. Now visualize the muscles in your thighs getting softer, letting go. Tell your legs to relax, to be still.

Keep breathing as you send a message to your hips and buttocks to release. Let the tension out; let them relax. Allow the feeling of relaxation to spread throughout your stomach and back like a warm glow. With each breath you feel calmer and stronger. Your stomach and back and legs and feet all feel very heavy, very relaxed. Concentrate now on your chest and shoulders. Let your lungs increase fully; now let them release fully. Let all the tightness in your chest go. Let your shoulder blades sink into the floor. Let gravity pull your spine and shoulders down towards the floor. Let all your

upper body relax. You're sinking into the floor. The floor will totally support you.

Feel all the tension slide past your shoulders and down your arms. Your arm muscles are relaxing and getting soft. Let all the tightness go. Relax your forearms, wrists, your hands. The tension is flooding out through your fingertips. Stop holding them up and in. Let them relax.

Now visualize the muscles that support your neck and head all day long. Tell them it's time to rest. Let the floor support you, it's time to relax. Release all the tightness in your throat. Allow the muscles in your chin, your cheeks, and your forehead to relax. Your face feels good. Feel the tension lift from your eyes, let the feeling of relaxation spread from your eyes, like rings of water spread around a stone. Relax. Time to rest. The muscles in your scalp are relaxing, your head feels loose and clear.

Your whole body can now relax as gravity pulls it towards the floor. Breathe in and out. Your heels, calves, thighs, shoulders, back, arms, hands, face, and head are very relaxed. Your whole body feels heavy, relaxed. Gravity will do all the work. Let your body go.

Now, with the body resting quietly, focus on your breath. Feel the soft air passing in and out, and the gentle rhythm of breath, like waves, coming in and going out. Inhale life-giving, quiet energy. Exhale worries and tension. Your body is resting quietly.

Breathe slowly and deeply. Concentrate on your breathing. Nothing is more important now than your breath and the quiet, calm feeling in your mind and body. You're very relaxed, but alert.

Remember this place, remember these feelings. Create a memory to use later when you need it. Remember: this feels good. Tell yourself, this feels good. Relaxation and quiet feel good.

It's time to come back now. Remember where you've been, then decide to come forward. Nourished and ready to return, begin by assuming control of your breathing. Take a good deep breath, spread energy throughout your system. Feeling positive, charged, visualize this new energy as it moves out from your center and spreads over your body. See it going down your arms into your hands—now let your fingers move.

Continue these deep energizing breaths. Take deep inhalations and strong exhalations, a bit faster than before. You need new energy. It's moving down the front of your body and into your legs. Now let your feet move. Feel this energy move into your face and head. Your body is ready to move. Arrive fully in the moment. Let your eyes open. Let a smile grow on your face as you sit up. Stretch…you feel good! Let's stand up now. You're done.

PROGRESSIVE RELAXATION SCRIPT #2

Begin by lying on your back with your eyes closed, hands at your sides, facing upwards. Let your feet fall apart naturally as you begin to breathe slowly and deeply. Take a long, deep inhalation, then release it with a sigh. You're starting to let go of all of your tension. You're going to allow yourself to relax.

As your body relaxes, you begin to feel gravity pressing you into the floor. Under your heels, calves, and thighs, you'll feel the weight of your legs. Under your buttocks, back, shoulders, and arms, the feeling of weight is pressing down. The floor will support you. Your head becomes heavier and heavier as the muscles in the back of your neck and face relax, soften, and release. Your whole body is heavy and relaxed, with the floor doing all the work of supporting you. Gravity does the work as the body lets go and allows itself to rest completely. Your mind is very alert. The body is resting quietly. Be still now, focus on your breathing; breathe through your nose in long, steady breaths.

Become aware of your hands now—first your right hand, then your left hand. Slowly let each hand tighten into a fist. Be careful to tense only the muscles in your hands and arms. Make those fists tight, but keep your face relaxed; your stomach and shoulders are loose. Tighter, tighter, as tight as possible, hold all the tension in those two fists; feel all the work, all the energy that's required to hold in that tension.

Now slowly relax your hands. Feel the tension gradually leaving your fingers. Feel your arms and hands loosening and softening. Continue to say (silently) to yourself, "Let go, relax; let go, relax, even after you have uncurled your hands and can no longer feel any tightness. Open your hands wide in a stretch, then allow them to return to a "normal" position. As your arms and hands again become heavy and relaxed, experience the difference between the work of holding, and the naturalness of letting go.

Lying still, body relaxed and calm, slowly tighten the muscles in your face. Tighten the muscles around your eyes, your forehead, your jaw, your mouth. Feel your expression scrunch up hard, getting tight, getting as tight as possible. It's uncomfortable, but just for a moment feel this tension and the cost in energy. Feel your lips and teeth. Your eyes, scalp, throat, and especially your forehead are aching, they're working so hard. Make sure the tension is contained just in the face, that the shoulder and stomach muscles are relaxed.

Ever so slowly and gradually, begin to release. Learn to experience tension leaving the muscles. Release this tension slowly, saying to yourself, "Let go, relax."

Forehead and eyes let go; mouth, jaw and scalp relax. Let go and relax, even after you can no longer feel any tightness in your face. The muscles in your face are soft and relaxed again. Your head is heavy and relaxed. Take a deep breath and exhale slowly, releasing any leftover tension. Another deep inhalation and long, slow exhalation, letting relaxation spread through your whole body.

Now pull your shoulders up toward your head. Take a deep inhalation and hold it, then tighten your stomach and back. Hold this tension. Your breathing will be shallow, but hold it. Make your shoulders, chest, stomach, and back as tight as possible. Again, be sure to contain the tension in these areas only. Your face, arms and hands, legs should remain calm and relaxed. Experience the tension in the trunk of your body. Make it tighter, tighter. Notice the difficulty with your breathing. This is how many people unknowingly carry tension in their bodies. Notice how much work is required to maintain this tightness, this unpleasant tension.

Again now, slowly release this tension, as slowly as you can. Feel the tension leaving your shoulders, your chest, your stomach, your back. Say to yourself, "Let go, relax; let go, relax." Feel the process of letting go, the return of natural breathing, the loosening and softening of your muscles. Keep letting go, even after your body feels relaxed. Take a long deep breath, then release it. No tensions now, just quiet. Focus on your breath.

On your next inhalation, let your buttocks begin to tighten along with your legs. Tighten your thighs and calves. Point your toes hard so your legs are rigid. Make the muscles in your seat and legs hard, but keep your face, shoulders, and other areas relaxed. Make your breathing soft and natural as you hold this tension in your lower body. Feel the tension in your feet, calves, thighs, and buttocks get tighter and tighter.

Ever so slowly, allow the tension to release a little at a time. Experience varying degrees of tension as you continue to release, saying to yourself, "Let go, relax." Feel your buttocks and thighs and calves and feet releasing, your toes coming up into a more normal position. Take a deep breath, hold it, then release, letting go of any remaining tension in your body. Again experience the heaviness in your body. Completely let go and feel waves of relaxation with each breath. Like a gentle, warm ocean wave that washes over you, starting from the soles of your feet up to your head and back, these waves of calmness and peace spread over you.

Remember how much work and discomfort there was in holding. Remember how restful and natural letting go was. Experience this calm in your body now. Remember what this place is like, to make your return easier. Quietly, focus on your breath now, the sound and sensation of your breath passing. Thoughts may come but do not attach to them; decide to stay focused on your breath. Your body is quiet; your mind is alert.

Prepare to return now by taking control of your breath. Make your breath stronger and quicker with each inhalation. Imagine with each breath that you're bringing fresh, positive energy into your body. With each exhalation, you're releasing old, tired energy. Feel the energy you have created flowing through your body, going down into your fingertips, going down to your toes. Another deep inhalation…move this new energy into your face, allowing your eyes to open and a smile to grow. One more deep inhalation, sit up, smile. The exercise has ended.

TEEN INVENTORY ON RELAXATION

We all need time to recharge our batteries and release tension. This inventory is a way to see how often we provide that time for ourselves. Use it as a way to get to know yourself better.

1 **Have you ever been deeply, totally, completely relaxed? (Exclude sleeping.) If so, what did it feel like to be this relaxed?**

_____

_____

_____

2 **How does this feeling of relaxation compare to the feeling of stress? Compare how your body feels when it's relaxed vs. stressed. Compare what your thinking is like; compare what your speech and your relationships with other people are like.**

_____

_____

_____

3 **Think back over the last twenty-four hours. Recall the periods of stress and the periods of relaxation. Concentrate now on the intervals in which you felt most relaxed. Typically what—or who—helps you to relax? During an average day, when do you feel most relaxed?**

_____

_____

_____

4 **Do you schedule relaxation times into your day? Do you routinely allow yourself some time to restore yourself? Why or why not?**

_____

_____

_____

5 **What value do you see to regular relaxation?**

_____

_____

_____

SESSION 2

GETTING TO KNOW THE BEAST

Overview

Stress in human beings is a biologically inherited response to any potentially threatening or challenging stimuli. The "fight-or-flight response" consists of a chain of psychological and physiological events; it can be provoked by thoughts, fears, or memories, as well as actual physical danger. In contrast to the uniform symptoms involved in the stress reaction, people vary significantly in what makes them feel threatened. With awareness, skills training, and practice, however, we can tame the beast that alarms us. As we understand the nature of the beast, we can acquire a sense of control over it. We can learn when to avoid unnecessary danger and how to prepare for inevitable challenges. We also can learn how society may influence our thinking about stress and ways to cope. In some instances, these influences need to be questioned and even rejected.

Overall Goals Relevant to This Session

After completing this session, participants should:

Know the difference between a state of stress and relaxed well-being.

Understand the origins and nature of stress and its effects on health and well-being.

Learner Outcomes

The purpose of this session is to help teens to:

1. Describe the physical manifestations of the stress reaction in humans.

2. Explain the relationship between stress levels, health, and performance.

3. Differentiate between, and provide examples of, three different kinds of stress situations.

4. Identify the cultural norms surrounding the management of stress.

Relevant Chapters in the Student Book

- Introduction (pp. 1–7)
- Part I, "Fighting Invisible Tigers" (pp. 11–19), all three sections

Agenda

In order to accomplish these outcomes, leaders need to:

1. Present a mini-lecture on the definition and nature of stress (15 minutes).

2. Discuss the relationship between stress levels, health, and performance (5 minutes).

3. Present a framework which distinguishes between three different stress situations, and elicit examples of each kind (20 minutes).

4. Discuss how society at large—and their own peer culture—influences how people react to the different stressors (10 minutes).

Resources and Materials

- Handout or overhead of "Relationship of Stress Level to Performance" (page 41)

- Handout or overhead of "Three Types of Stress Situations" (page 42)

- Overhead projector and screen (optional)

- Chalkboard or easel pad (optional)

Activities

1. Present a mini-lecture on stress.

Ask teens how they would define stress. If appropriate, see if they can recall and elaborate upon the material in the student book. Differentiate between a *stressor*, which is the event, person, or task (the "tiger") which threatens us, and the *stress reaction*— the emotional and physical sensations we experience as a result of the stressor. What we typically call stress is the response to "any action or situation that places special physical or psychological demands on us."[1] David Elkind describes stress as "an excessive demand for adjustment that can arise from within or from without ourselves."[2] In order for the physiological and psychological response to occur, we have to mentally perceive the stressor as dangerous. The more dangerous we perceive a situation to be, and the less able we are to control or prepare for it, the greater our stress response.

Describe what's happening to the body during acute stress by explaining the fight-or-flight syndrome. On a simple level, stress can be seen in two stages. In stage 1, we go into temporary "shock." The heartbeat slows and becomes irregular, blood pressure and body temperature drop. Muscles go temporarily slack. In stage 2, "countershock" sets in. The aforementioned symptoms are reversed and actually increased as the body prepares to defend itself. Some of the key points in this syndrome are:[3]

- A stress-related neurochemical called *noradrenaline* is released in the nucleus of the brainstem.

- The noradrenaline quickly travels throughout the brain's branching nerve fibers and into the spinal cord.

- The sympathetic nerve cells of the nervous system accelerate the heart beat and stimulate the adrenal glands, which in turn produce more adrenaline that circulates the blood faster.

- As the heart speeds up, the body heats up, resulting in perspiration, rapid breathing, increased energy reserves, and muscular tension.

Ask students why this response might be useful to cave dwellers and animals. How would these physical changes prepare someone to either fight or flee? How useful is this type of physiological response to us today? Elicit examples.

2. Relate stress level to health and performance.

While the immediate strength and energy afforded by the stress reaction are helpful to us in dealing with immediate stressors, repeated or chronic stress begins to have a debilitating effect. Interestingly enough, researchers in the health professions have begun to look seriously at the relationship of illness to stress only in recent decades. The connection seems intuitively obvious; a body in constant stimulation, preparing for battle or flight, is repeatedly draining itself of vital resources, and thus has fewer resources with which to protect itself from disease. Professionals in nearly every health field, from nursing to internal medicine to psychiatry to dentistry to nutritional science, are exploring these correlations.

Currently, stress is believed to be a major factor in coronary artery disease, stomach ulcers, colitis, chronic backaches, headaches, and muscular tension. Two very stressful situations, the death of a spouse or the onset of a serious depression, are associated with illness.[4] Because stress depletes the body's resources, it lowers the body's resistance both to cold viruses and to more serious infectious diseases like pneumonia. Prolonged stress weakens the body's entire immune system, and may trigger or exacerbate illnesses such as cancer, multiple sclerosis, diabetes, and rheumatoid arthritis. Stress almost certainly underlies, or contributes to behavioral problems, such as the eating disorders of obesity, bulimia, and anorexia, as well as alcoholism and drug addiction. With its accompanying hormonal secretions, stress is even believed to be a prime contributor to acne flare-ups!

Although the extra power and heat caused by the fight-or-flight response enabled the cave dweller to fight more aggressively, or flee more successfully, today "many components of the stress response in humans work to shorten rather than lengthen a person's life span."[5] Even in the short term, the benefits of the stress reaction reach a vanishing point.

Show students the handout or overhead, "Relationship of Stress Level to Performance" (page 41). Explain that the term "performance" is being used broadly here and refers to any sporting, social, academic, musical, or dramatic performance. In moderate or controlled amounts, stress can help us perform at our best. It arouses us, increases our alertness, and provides us with energy. As stress and anxiety mount to an intolerable level, however, our performance begins to disintegrate. A singer, for example, won't be able to sing well if she gets a dry mouth from rapid breathing, or if her diaphragm is too tense too expand to capacity. A sense of fatigue, disorganization, and inattention takes over with prolonged stress, making concentration, memory recall, physical coordination, even visual perception difficult. If you are lost in a strange city and driving in the dark in a thunderstorm, you may be unable to read a simple street sign or remember whether you are supposed to turn right or left.

The ability to process new information or to remember previously learned material is particularly affected when we're under too much stress. Moderating stress is therefore a critical skill for students, new employees, and practically anyone in a learning situation. Stress management involves both knowing when to avoid foreseeable stress, and preparing for unavoidable stress.

3. Differentiate between stress situations and elicit examples for each.

Some interesting research on stress indicates that several factors affect our perception of the severity of stress, other than the awesomeness of the "tiger" itself. Two of the most significant of these factors are whether a person 1) feels any control over the amount or type of stress, or 2) receives any advance warning of danger or pain. Control over the source of stress appears to delay or prevent people from disintegrating under pressure. Similarly, being able to

predict or prepare for stress enhances a person's stability during stress.

David Elkind[6] distinguishes between three stress situations (see also the handout or overhead, "Three Types of Stress Situations," on page 42):

■ Foreseeable and Avoidable

This kind of stressor can be foreseen. It can also be avoided.

Examples: A roller coaster ride, a Steven King thriller, or a walk through a dangerous neighborhood; skydiving, taking the lead in a school play, or going on a blind date. Unfortunately, many of the foreseeable and avoidable stressors look attractive to teens, especially to those who are bent on taking risks or testing limits. Drinking, using drugs, playing hooky, etc., all invite conflict as well as direct adverse consequences (e.g., throwing up, AIDS from dirty needles, missing assignments due to absences). Some of these stressors gain social approval and support from peer groups, while at the same time earning disapproval from adults.

■ Unforeseeable and Unavoidable

This kind of stressor is neither foreseeable nor avoidable.

Examples: Community or peer violence; accidents not resulting from any negligence or recklessness; the death of a beloved pet, friend, or family member; the divorce or separation of one's parents; relocation to a new city and new school due to a change in a parent's job. Typically, there is considerable sympathy and support for this kind of stress, because the person did not "invite" it.

■ Foreseeable but Unavoidable

This kind of stressor can be foreseen, but it can't be avoided.

Examples: Final exams; first dates; job interviews; meeting your mom's new boyfriend; changes in appearance due to puberty. It can be tempting for outsiders to minimize inevitable stressors, because "we all have to go through them." Nonetheless, they can sap much adolescent energy.

Show the "Three Types of Stress Situations" overhead (page 42) and have teens classify some of the various stressors in their lives according to the framework.

4. Discuss the adult and peer cultural norms surrounding stress management.

Ask students what messages they have heard, and perhaps internalized over the years, regarding how people are supposed to react in stressful situations and how to manage stress generally. Use examples generated in #1 above to focus your questions.

American culture is strongly rooted in the work ethic and individualism of the pioneer. These traditions, while "building a great nation," tend to place a heavy burden on individuals to make or break it on their own and to succeed at any price. Our competitive spirit, which goes hand-in-hand with a free market economy, extends now to almost every facet of our lives, including parenting.

In order to prepare children to compete successfully in social and economic circles, for example, parents have begun to program kids from an early age in academic activities, music, the arts, and sports.[7] Some children never have any free time, even in the summer, to learn how to make up their own plays, build forts, and develop other social activities. Kids no longer organize their own after-school baseball or kickball games, for example; youth sports have become highly organized with professional coaches, uniforms, travel schedules, and try-outs. This turns *play*, which is stress-reducing and relationship-building, into *work*, which can be so stressful that kids stop participating in sports (or other parent-run endeavors) by the time they get to high school. A survey in 1987 of 26,300 10-to-18-year-olds found that by age 15, 75% of those who had played a youth sport no longer played it, primarily because "it's not fun anymore," but also because "there is so much emphasis on winning by the coaches and the parents that nothing else seems to matter."[8]

Questions which may stimulate a good discussion of the cultural norms surrounding stress are:

■ Do young women and men act differently during crises? How so? Does society seem to permit them to act differently?

■ Do young men and women get stressed out by the same things? If not, what do young men typically

get stressed out about? What do young women get stressed out about?

■ What messages does our society give about the concept of "free time"? Is free time good? How much is acceptable? What is supposed to happen during free time?

■ Is America "in love with winning"? Are we more competitive than other nations? Why or why not? What's wrong with losing?

■ Is showing stress a sign of weakness? Why or why not? Why are things which some people do to moderate stress (such as yoga, relaxation exercises, aerobic exercise) considered alternatives to "regular" medicine? Why aren't they considered prerequisites for health?

■ Why does the term "psychosomatic illness" usually denigrate a person's disease in society's eyes?

Questions that may get at the norms of the adolescent peer culture include these:

■ Do you tend to give people more support when they are experiencing unforeseeable, unavoidable stress than when they are experiencing stress that can be foreseen and avoided? Why or why not?

■ Have you ever been encouraged or inclined to accept a risk that you didn't want to take? How did you handle that? Did you go along, or decide the risk wasn't worth it?

■ How can you tell which stressors are "good for you" vs. those that are "bad for you"?

Suggestions for Other Activities and Projects

■ As an alternative to lecturing on the origins and nature of stress, show the film "Stress and the Emotions" from the public television series *The Brain.* Check your local video store or public library. This is an hour-long segment, so some prescreening and partial showing may be necessary.

■ If a science teacher or psychologist is one of the co-leaders, he or she could contribute many more examples of the research being conducted on the stress response itself, and on the effects of stress on psychological and physical health. For those of you near a library system, there is a vast literature on stress in medicine, nursing, and public health. Bill Moyers's book, *Healing and the Mind* (see "References" below), considers some of the best research currently going on in areas such as biofeedback, yoga, and group therapy, and also the basic research on the neuropsychobiological components of stress and the body/mind connections.

■ Have teens group themselves into teams. Have each team develop a list of ten situations that create stress.

■ Assign participants an individual writing project on this theme: "Compose a story in which stress helped you in some way."

■ Have nurses come to your group to explain blood pressure and demonstrate how blood pressure is checked.

REFERENCES

1. Restak, R. *The Brain.* (New York: Bantam Books, 1984), p. 166.

2. Elkind, David. *All Grown Up and No Place to Go.* (Reading, MA: Addison-Wesley Publishing Co., 1984), p. 160.

3. Restak, R. Ibid., pp. 164–165.

4. Moyers, Bill. *Healing and the Mind.* (New York: Doubleday, 1993.)

5. Restak, R. Ibid., p. 165.

6. Elkind, D. Ibid., pp. 165–168.

7. Ibid., chapters 1 and 5.

8. Anderson, C. *Keeping Youth Sports Safe and Fun.* (Minneapolis: Minnesota Children's Trust Fund, 1994.) For copies of this booklet, write or call: Minnesota Amateur Sports Commission, 1700–15th Avenue NE, Blaine, MN 55434; (612) 785-5630.

RELATIONSHIP OF STRESS LEVEL TO PERFORMANCE

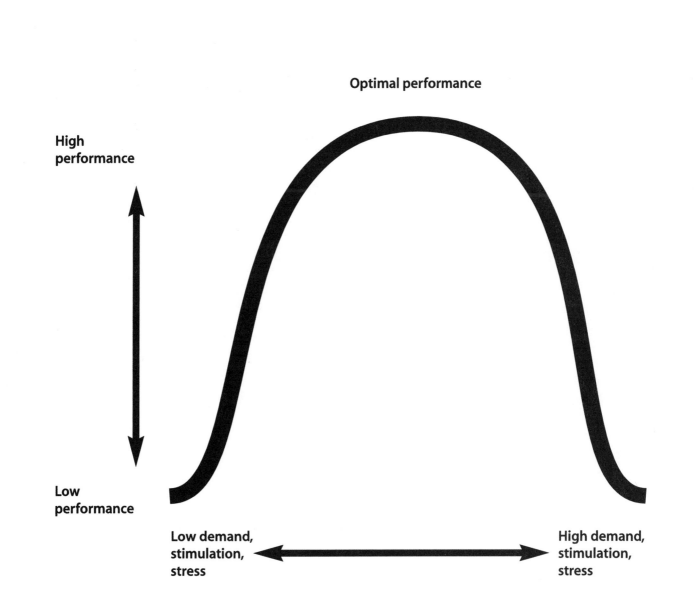

Optimal performance

High performance

Low performance

Low demand, stimulation, stress ⟷ **High demand, stimulation, stress**

THREE TYPES OF STRESS SITUATIONS

Psychologist David Elkind suggests that there are three basic kinds of stress situations: Foreseeable/Avoidable, Unforeseeable/Unavoidable, and Foreseeable/Avoidable. How would you classify the following situations? In which "box" would you put each one?

Hitchhiking	Auditions	Physical changes of puberty
A final exam	First date	Breaking curfew
Death of a pet	Parent's divorce	Unprotected sex
Illness	Parent's expectations	Getting a "bad" teacher

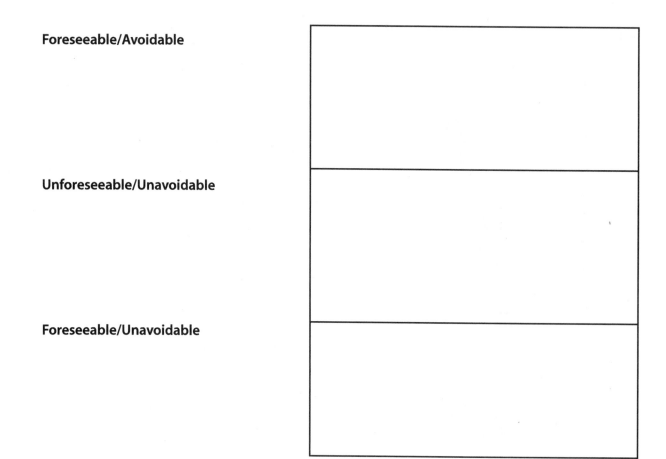

Foreseeable/Avoidable

Unforeseeable/Unavoidable

Foreseeable/Unavoidable

What are some other examples of these three kinds of stress? Do you think there is such a thing as Unforeseeable but Avoidable stress (the fourth possible box)? Why or why not?

The labels for the three types of stress situations are from Elkind, D., *All Grown Up and No Place to Go* (Reading, MA: Addison-Wesley Publishing Co., 1984), pp. 165–168.

PART II

WHEN THE

TIGER BITES

SESSION 3

FIRST AID: COPING VS. STRESS MANAGEMENT

Overview

When people haven't identified the triggers that distress them, or the habits they unconsciously perpetuate that increase stress, they're likely to feel somewhat paralyzed when sudden challenges arise. Their first instinct may be to adopt whatever short-term strategies distract them or dull the pain. We call this "coping."

Coping is a natural survival mechanism. Some coping strategies are effective in the short term, but the essence of even positive coping is the avoidance of feeling; the root causes of stress are not addressed. Too much coping can be destructive and lead to a "crashing and burning" style of existence. In this session, participants look at common teen stressors and signs of stress, and identify positive and negative coping strategies. Participants complete a self-inventory and graph the short-term benefits and consequences of various coping strategies.

Overall Goals Relevant to This Session

After completing this session, participants should:

Understand the origins and nature of stress and its effects on health and well-being.

Be able to evaluate current stressors, stress levels, and methods of coping.

Learner Outcomes

The purpose of this session is to help teens to:

1. Relate common teen stressors and stress symptoms to their own situations.

2. Distinguish between coping and stress management, and between positive and negative coping strategies.

3. Evaluate their own stress levels and consequences of coping strategies.

Relevant Chapters in the Student Book

■ Part I, "Tropical Illusions" (pp. 20–25) and "How Teenagers Cope with Stress" (pp. 26–36)

Agenda

In order to accomplish these outcomes, leaders need to:

1. After teens complete a self-inventory, lead a group discussion on common teen stressors and stress symptoms (25 minutes).

2. Lead a group discussion in which teens distinguish between coping and stress management, and graph the effects of positive and negative coping strategies (25 minutes).

Resources and Materials

■ Handout of "Teen Inventory on Common Stressors and Stress Symptoms" (pages 47–50)

■ Overhead projector and screen (optional)

■ Chalkboard or easel pad (optional)

■ Handout or overhead of "Sample Graph of Stress and Coping Strategies" (page 51) (optional)

■ Handout of "Measuring Emotional Stress" (pages 117–120) (optional)

Activities

1. Discuss teen stressors and stress symptoms.

Pass around the handout, "Teen Inventory on Common Stressors and Stress Symptoms" (pages 47–50). Although participants should not be required to hand in the inventory, ask them to complete it for their own use. Tell them that the information comes from observations made by psychologists and teachers working with young people. Ask teens if they feel the lists do a good job of capturing the kinds of stressors they experience. Ask them to brainstorm with you: What else should go on the list? Other possible discussion questions:

■ Do you think the stressors listed here are permanent? Or are they likely to change over time? Explain.

■ How do these stressors compare with those you observe operating in other people's lives? Do adults seem to have different stressors?

■ Does this inventory help you identify areas of possible stress for yourself that you weren't aware of previously?

■ What is your most typical symptom of stress? How does stress most consistently affect you?

2. Lead a discussion on coping strategies.

Ask teens to clarify the difference between the common forms of coping listed in the student book. The three major categories of coping are *distractions*, *avoidance*, and *escape*. Ask teens to provide typical examples of each, and to say what is positive or negative about the strategy.

■ *Distractions* include watching television, eating, taking a bath, reading a book. Distractions are relatively harmless but also the shortest-lived and least potent method of coping.

■ *Avoidance* tactics are distractions in the extreme: constantly wearing headphones (even during class or meal times) is an example. Avoidance tactics usually allow the problem to become

bigger, which triggers more avoidance, thus becoming a vicious circle. Excessive sleep, procrastination, even illness can be signs of avoidance.

■ *Escapist behaviors* are distraction and avoidance measures taken to the extreme. They are a signal that the limits of coping have been reached, and the person wants "out." Skipping school, running away from home, and abusing drugs or alcohol are means of escape with serious consequences.

You may need to reinforce the difference between positive and negative coping strategies. Positive methods of "quick relief" include going for a walk after an argument at home, doing some relaxation or deep breathing before an exam, and getting rid of tension by engaging in physical activity. Examples of negative coping strategies can include tactics like those listed above, but done to the extreme: walking for six hours in the dead of night, doing deep breathing before every class, or jogging seven days a week for three hours a day. These are signs that coping strategies are being pushed to unreasonable limits. Over-intellectualizing or rationalizing a problem can also do more harm than good if it constitutes a person's prevailing method of stress management. Finally, certain coping strategies (e.g., drinking, promiscuity) quickly become destructive as they create bigger and bigger problems.

Try graphing on a chalkboard (or use the sample graph on page 51 as a handout or overhead) the effects on our stress levels when we use various coping strategies. Your graph might look similar to the graphs on pages 15 and 19 of the student book. The purpose is to have participants visually appreciate how a coping strategy (such as avoidance) only takes care of the problem for a little while. Ultimately, an ineffective strategy creates its own stress.

This can happen, for example, when the reaction to a difficult homework assignment is to put it off until the last moment. During the period of time when the homework could be broken down into small, manageable steps, the student probably feels some initial relief: he or she isn't thinking about the difficult project. As the time of the project's due date gets closer, the anxiety mounts. On the due date, a second avoidance strategy is tried: the student "forgets" the work and can't turn it in on time. Momentarily, the threat of being judged is delayed. Next week,

he same subject matter is given.
, because the student is not
third avoidance strategy is tried:
a brief period, the student once
again …   relief from stress, because he or she
is out in the hall or out of the building, not thinking
about the test. This hiatus is interrupted, of course,
when the grade report comes out. The poor showing
leads to a fight with parents, loss of car privileges,
and sense of failure—a lot of stress.

The "ups" and "downs" of this kind of cycle, which
escalates over time, could be depicted with a number
of examples. Procrastination and avoidance are
perhaps the most common, but somewhat subtle examples of inappropriate teenage coping strategies. Others
that are more dramatic (and obvious?) include:

■ *Sex.* Sex can feel great at the moment. It can
temporarily release a lot of bodily tension and
ease many emotional fears and pains. Some of the
consequences of premature sex, however, are
increased stress and anxiety due to guilt one feels
later; insecurity about your partner's loyalty; fear
of getting pregnant (or impregnating a partner),
or actually getting pregnant; fear of contracting a
sexually transmitted disease, or actually
contracting a disease.

■ *Drinking.* Alcohol is an infamous mechanism for
releasing inhibitions and removing oneself from
the worries and demands of the day. Some of the
consequences of drinking, which raise the stress
level and thereby create a vicious cycle, include
guilt, disorientation (due to memory loss or
missed appointments, incomplete assignments),
backlash from other friends who may have been
disturbed from your drunkenness, fines from
having destroyed property or been caught for
speeding, loss of driver's license, etc.

■ *Aggressive Behavior.* Acting out violently makes
one feel temporarily powerful and in control. Yet

the consequences of such behavior—e.g., driving
recklessly, daring oneself or others to do
dangerous things, fighting, vandalism—can have
tragic consequences.

■ *Any Extreme Activity.* Compulsive eating is an
example of a normally healthy activity which,
carried to the extreme, is unhealthy. Initially, food
can provide comfort; uncontrolled overeating
leads to unhappy physical and social outcomes.

Complete the session by reiterating the need for
lifeskills as an alternative to inappropriate coping
strategies.

Suggestions for Other Activities and Projects

■ Invite participants to share with each other what
they learned about their own stress levels in small
groups, or in a journal exercise.

■ As an alternative to "Teen Inventory on Common
Stressors and Stress Symptoms" (pages 47–50),
use the "Measuring Emotional Stress" questionnaire (pages 117–120). Developed by the
University of Minnesota Adolescent Health
Program, this questionnaire was based on items
used to measure emotional stress in a large
statewide survey. Copies of the entire youth
survey, as well as related monograph reports and
publications, are available from the National
Adolescent Health Resource Center (telephone:
612/627-4488). The authors of this survey invite
questions and encourage others to conduct practical research with this instrument, and are very
helpful in working with practitioners interested
in doing so.

TEEN INVENTORY ON COMMON STRESSORS AND STRESS SYMPTOMS

Use this self-inventory to gauge the amount of stress in your life. It is not a scientific instrument; there is no official score. Rather, simply count up the number of "symptoms" you have experienced in the last month, and the number of stressors that apply to you, and reflect on whether this number seems manageable or not. You may want to keep this inventory and review it in six weeks to see whether your stressors are more or less numerous, or your stress symptoms more or less severe. The results may also suggest a particular stressor or stress symptoms to focus on and improve.

Today's Date: _____

STRESS SYMPTOMS

Circle the degree to which you have experienced the following symptoms in the previous month. Circle 0 (zero) if you haven't experienced the symptom to any degree. Circle 1 if you have experienced the symptom to a minor degree, circle 2 for a moderate degree, and circle 3 if you have experienced the symptom to a major degree.

SYMPTOM	NONE			MAJOR
Chronic dissatisfaction	0	1	2	3
Loss of interest or pleasure	0	1	2	3
Excessive sleeping or sleeplessness	0	1	2	3
Always irritable, angry over small things	0	1	2	3
Reject positive comments or support from others	0	1	2	3
Difficulty concentrating	0	1	2	3
Major change in academic performance	0	1	2	3
Significant change in eating habits	0	1	2	3
Ongoing, recurrent worries	0	1	2	3
Nightmares or disturbing dreams	0	1	2	3
Increase in the number of mishaps, accidents	0	1	2	3
Obsessive-compulsive about routines, time, dress, grades, etc.	0	1	2	3
Jittery, hyper	0	1	2	3
Withdrawal, aversion	0	1	2	3
Recurrent physical ailments (headaches, colds, etc.)	0	1	2	3

➡️

Teen Inventory on Common Stressors continued

STRESSORS

*Circle **Y** ("YES") or **N** ("NO") as appropriate for all the items below. Circle **Y** if you've experienced stress (see symptoms above) related to the item in the last month.*

Stressors at Home

Arguments with parent(s) or other adult at home	Y	N
Conflicts with brother(s) or sister(s)	Y	N
Significant change in family, such as:		
■ Separation or divorce of parents	Y	N
■ Blending of two families (moving in with step-siblings)	Y	N
■ Remarriage of a parent	Y	N
■ Parent changes jobs	Y	N
■ At-home parent gets a full-time job outside of the home	Y	N
Move to a new house or apartment	Y	N
Home remodeling—invasion of your "space"	Y	N
Alcohol or drug abuse by family member	Y	N
Physical or sexual abuse by a family member of a sibling or other	Y	N
Physical or sexual abuse by a family member of yourself	Y	N
Parent or family member becomes seriously ill	Y	N
Parent or family member dies	Y	N
A pet dies	Y	N

Stressors at School

Did less well in school (academically) than expected or desired	Y	N
Underwent educational or psychological testing	Y	N
Placed in special class (gifted, remedial, other)	Y	N
Had confrontation with teacher, coach, or administrative staff	Y	N
Was tardy for three or more classes	Y	N
Was expelled from a class	Y	N

From *A Leader's Guide to Fighting Invisible Tigers* by Connie C. Schmitz, Ph.D., with Earl Hipp, copyright © 1995. Free Spirit Publishing Inc, Minneapolis, MN; 866/703-7322; *www.freespirit.com*. This page may be photocopied for individual classroom or small group work only.

Teen Inventory on Common Stressors continued

From *A Leader's Guide to Fighting Invisible Tigers* by Connie C. Schmitz, Ph.D., with Earl Hipp, copyright © 1995. Free Spirit Publishing Inc., Minneapolis, MN; 866/703-7322; *www.freespirit.com*. This page may be photocopied for individual classroom or small group work only.

	Y	N
Received a detention	Y	N
Received probation for academic or behavioral problem	Y	N
Felt frustrated with learning	Y	N
Was singled out for an award or special recognition	Y	N
Was elected to an honored position (captain, editor)	Y	N
Was accepted to or promoted on an athletic team	Y	N
Was eliminated from or demoted on an athletic team	Y	N
Incidents of school vandalism occurred at your school	Y	N
Incidents of youth violence occurred at school or neighborhood	Y	N
Other disruptions in school (e.g., teacher's strike, resignation of principal, change in class size, school closings)	Y	N

Stressors with Peers

	Y	N
Fell in love with someone new	Y	N
Lost a significant friend due to relocation or separation	Y	N
Felt your trust or confidence was betrayed by a significant friend	Y	N
Became disillusioned with a previous girlfriend or boyfriend	Y	N
Was "dropped" by a boyfriend or girlfriend you really care for	Y	N
No longer feel part of the same old crowd	Y	N
Don't have a group that you feel comfortable hanging out with	Y	N
Excluded from groups that you'd like to be part of	Y	N
Feel less adequate, compared to your friends	Y	N
Feel your friends make too many demands on you	Y	N
Engaged in unprotected sex with partner	Y	N
Became pregnant, or impregnated a partner	Y	N

Stressors with Self

	Y	N
Concerned about weight, height, physical development	Y	N
Concerned about clothes, other material things	Y	N
Change in employment or income status	Y	N

Teen Inventory on Common Stressors continued

Wondered what you are "good at" .... Y   N

Questioned what your future will be.. Y   N

Passed (or failed) your driver's test.. Y   N

Went through bar/bat mitzvah training or religious confirmation .... Y   N

Received acceptance (or rejection) from college... Y   N

Conflict over major decisions involving values, life choices...................................... Y   N

Used alcohol or drugs .... Y   N

Dealing with issues of homosexuality and self... Y   N

Dealing with chronic illness or disability .... Y   N

Considered leaving home, moving out on your own .... Y   N

Stressors Related to Life

Questioned whether God exists, what religion means to you .... Y   N

Felt injustice in your immediate world (e.g., racism, sexism) .... Y   N

Felt environmental threats in your immediate world .... Y   N

Loss of influential adult in your life (other than a parent).. Y   N

Negative images in the media (violence, sexuality, stereotyping, etc.) .... Y   N

Lack of challenge in life: not much to do, not many places to go .... Y   N

Lack of community: disconnectedness in neighborhood, school .... Y   N

Lack of economic opportunity, money.. Y   N

Overwhelming sense of authority, structure, conformity, no options...................... Y   N

From A *Leader's Guide to Fighting Invisible Tigers* by Connie C. Schmitz, Ph.D., with Earl Hipp, copyright © 1995. Free Spirit Publishing Inc., Minneapolis, MN; 866/703-7322; *www.freespirit.com.* This page may be photocopied for individual classroom or small group work only.

SAMPLE GRAPH OF STRESS AND COPING STRATEGIES

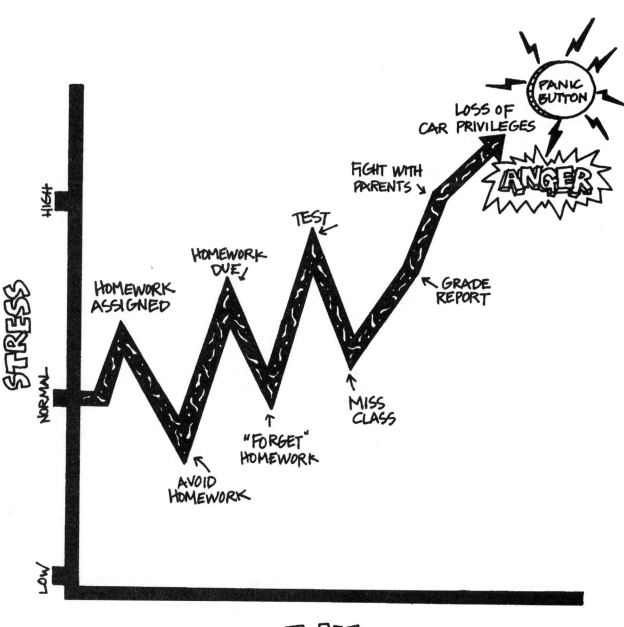

SESSION 4

REACHING LIMITS, REACHING OUT

Overview

In this last session on stress itself, we help teens deal with the fact that even the best coping strategies—even the best lifeskills—won't always protect us from feeling extreme stress at some point during our lives. Some stress is unbearable. These situations call for immediate help from trusted adults. What can we do for ourselves and our friends when situations reach crisis level?

Because this one session cannot substitute for more far-reaching group therapy, it is not intended to be confrontational. That is, participants are not expected to "bare their souls" in confession, although some sharing of personal problems may come out. Rather, the session is designed to give teens permission to seek help—from each other and from other adults and professionals—if problems have become too big to handle. This happens first in hearing "stories" of six hypothetical teens who haven fallen into a pattern of dealing with stressful lives with some not-so-successful coping strategies. Later in the session, participants identify a stressor they can and need to resolve by writing it down on a piece of paper and then tearing the paper into shreds. One by one, they come forward to the center of the room and deal privately with this "tiger" by ripping it into pieces.

Because young people in crisis are not necessarily the ones sitting in front of you, this session also tries to support the many teens who are doing okay themselves, but have friends, siblings, or acquaintances in crisis. Teens don't necessarily know what to do or say when others are on the edge, heading into trouble, about to make decisions which they know are bad. What do you say to someone who has mistakenly dealt with stress by turning to drugs, running away from home, or becoming anorexic?

How do you get an adult involved if you feel a friend is suicidal? In a small group exercise, participants generate lists of "20 Things to Say or Do for a Friend in Crisis." In some cases, these will be messages they can take to their own heart, as well.

Overall Goals Relevant to This Session

After completing this session, participants should:

Be able to evaluate current stressors, stress levels, and methods of coping.

Feel empowered to care for themselves and seek help and support when needed.

Learner Outcomes

The purpose of this session is to help teens to:

1. Identify stress thresholds which indicate some immediate help is needed.

2. Develop knowledge and skills in how to support other teens in crisis.

3. Identify tigers in their own lives which may need "outside" help.

Relevant Chapters in the Student Book

■ Part II, "Self-Care for Tiger Bites" (pp. 37–49)

Agenda

In order to accomplish these outcomes, leaders need to:

1. Profile six different coping patterns commonly used by teens (15 minutes).

2. Lead a small group exercise in which teens identify positive ways to support friends (and themselves) in crisis (20 minutes).

3. Lead an activity in which teens identify a stressor in their own lives and mentally address this tiger and "let it go" (15 minutes).

Resources and Materials

- Script, "Six Coping Styles of Teens in Stress" (pages 55–56)

- Handout of "20 Things to Say or Do for a Friend in Crisis" (page 57)

- Chalkboard or easel pad

- Trash receptacle (perhaps a specially labeled box) for disposing of torn paper

- Candle, matches, and flameproof bowl or metal trash container (optional)

Activities

1. Relate six profiles of coping behavior.

Psychologist David Elkind[1] summarizes how adolescents who have not yet integrated their identity with the demands and expectations of society tend to react when faced with stressful situations. The hallmark characteristics of these "patchwork" personalities in the face of stress are 1) anxious, 2) conforming, 3) self-punishing, 4) obsessively competitive, 5) angry, and 6) fearful. Based on the characteristics outlined by Elkind, we have written six hypothetical profiles, "Six Coping Styles of Teens in Stress" (pages 55–56). These six profiles can be related as stories to illustrate how people who are not using lifeskills react to stress in their lives. This provides another way for teens to possibly identify their own pattern, to "see" themselves without being confronted too directly or openly. After presenting the profiles, the main questions to have the participants think about are:

- Are these teens in trouble? What are they doing and/or not doing?

- What do you think will happen to them? Will their "strategies" work?

- Is it time to get help? Why or why not?

As you read or narrate these profiles, write the six category labels (e.g., "Anxious") on the board, so that by the end, all six labels are listed.

2. Lead a small group exercise in problem-solving.

Divide the teens into small groups for the next task. Having talked about the six profiles, introduce the notion that sometime in our lives we all will be faced with the problem of having a friend or loved one in trouble. For many of us, that has already happened. We need to know that we don't have to be silent on the sidelines. We can offer support; we can guide a friend to help; we can be firm in not supporting a strategy which hurts a friend's self-esteem, relationships, options, or long-term health.

Once in their small groups, participants are to share stories of situations where friends (or themselves, if they desire) have reached the limits of their coping. Then they are to generate lists of "20 Things to Say or Do for a Friend in Crisis," using the handout on page 57. In preparing these lists, participants can draw upon advice offered in the student book, or from their own experience and wisdom. At the end of the exercise, groups share their top five ideas with the larger group. Alternatively, lists can be turned in to the leader, typed up and duplicated, and redistributed to the large group at the next session.

3. Lead an activity in letting go of unnecessary stress.

As seen in Session 2, some stressors are not under our control, while others are. Even with unforeseeable and unavoidable stressors, however, our perceptions influence how much actual stress we feel. There is, in nearly every situation—no matter how awful—a way to mentally reframe the situation and to adjust the amount of stress we feel by changing our perspective or expectations. Perhaps we are angry about a "tiger" that, in reality, disappeared many years ago. Perhaps by seeing the tiger from another perspective, we realize he is not as big as we thought he was. Perhaps the tiger simply needs to be told to stay in his place; we acknowledge him, and will deal with him, but we refuse to be afraid of him or do battle with him every waking minute and hour of the day. All this helps us to gain some control over the stressor. It may mean putting something behind us that is over and done with (e.g., forgive and forget). It may mean committing to confront something or somebody that has been lurking in the bushes and we weren't able to face directly. It may mean going to get help from trusted adults or older friends. It may mean preparing to defend ourselves more proactively in the future. Whatever the tiger is, the threat can be minimized by our own mental attitude. We have some power over our anxious, conforming, self-punishing, competitive, angry, and fearful behavior.

A symbolic way to gain a sense of control over a stressor is to name it, label it, write it down on a piece of paper, and then tear it to shreds. (Or, if fire regulations permit lighting a candle, the paper can be burned and dropped into a flameproof bowl or metal trash container.) This is one way to say, "I have allowed this threat to be part of me, to preoccupy me (perhaps subconsciously), but no longer. Today I have named it, and have resolved to do something about it."

To make this symbolic gesture meaningful, it helps if a respectful period of silence is established as participants privately identify their tigers. Then, individually, teens come forward to the center of the room, tear up their "tigers," and drop their torn paper into a special trash receptacle. You may suggest (or role model it, by going first) that the individuals voice words of resolve as they tear up their paper and drop it into the container. Suggested examples:

- "I hereby resolve to do something about this tiger today."

- "I am no longer helpless in the face of this stressor."

- "This stressor is history."

- "I can let go of this stressor."

Depending upon the group, appropriate reactions to each teen may include simple hugs, smiles, a pat on the back, or affirmations, such as: "Way to go, Anna."

Conclude the session with statements that reinforce the power each of us has over our stressors and stress reactions. Sharing problems with a friend or adult is always a good idea, and never a sign of weakness. Beginning with Session 5, we hope to further empower participants by broadening their knowledge and competence with various lifeskills.

Suggestions for Other Activities and Projects

- Have a referral list ready to distribute at the end of this session. Include the names of professional counselors, school-based clinics, city or county agencies, hotlines, religious organizations, and other sources of help for teens and their families. Provide your phone number on it, or circulate a business card, if you wish to make yourself available to participants after the session. It would be worth your while to do a fair amount of research of this list ahead of time, and to think creatively about the different places where young people could get some support. You might also want to circulate a reading list for teens who are experiencing significant problems.

- Have a "guest speaker" (e.g., former drug user, teen mother) come speak to the class about their personal experiences with risk behaviors and the sources of stress they have identified in their lives.

- Choose passages from famous novels, autobiographies, or diaries which capture the feeling that a crisis is overwhelming the main character. What might work best are first-person stories of people who later came to some resolution of a problem. Example: Maya Angelou's experience running away and getting pregnant as a teenager, after having been sexually abused as a child, in *I Know Why the Caged Bird Sings*. Get some suggestions from the English teacher of other famous autobiographies.

Recommended Reading

■ Moyers, Bill. *Healing and the Mind.* (New York: Doubleday, 1993.)

REFER

1. Elkind, David. *All Grown U[...]*
(Reading, MA: Addison-We[...]
pp. 168–177.

SIX COPING STYLES OF TEENS IN STRESS

ANXIOUS

Garret is always worrying. When he opens his mouth, it's usually to say something sarcastic or negative, like "Yeah, right, our team is going to beat South High." But often he doesn't talk. When at home, he goes into his room and closes the door and stays there all night, coming out only for dinner. When at school, he avoids situations where he might get angry or look stupid. Before a school debate last year, he felt so nervous he literally got sick—rather, he *felt* sick, although the doctor said it was just a cold or something, and not to worry. Even on days when he feels fine, he has a hard time getting up in the morning. Things are so boring, he feels incredibly tired most of the day. What really bothers him is when he's under pressure to make decisions or choices. Who should he invite to homecoming? What should he wear to the dance? Ought he attend the basketball game tonight, when a science quiz is scheduled for the next day? With all the possible things that could go wrong that could make him look foolish, it is really hard to take action.

CONFORMING

Betsy and Jana are twins, but they are opposites in every way but one. They are both conforming—going along with things to gain approval and acceptance—but they have chosen different models to go along with. Betsy is aggressively popular with the "fast" kids. At thirteen, she's done most things she thinks adults or popular kids do. She's tried marijuana and cocaine, she drinks beer with the guys, she's gone "all the way" with her boyfriend. Last year she had her nose pierced, just like the punkers who hang out at the mall. These accomplishments have earned her a solid place in the "in" crowd. Sister Jana has chosen a very different path. She is so impossibly good, she does everything she is told. Her parents obviously prefer her to Betsy; she's home most weekend nights, studying. Her dad still calls her "My little Jana." Jana has never missed an assignment, or gone to school unprepared, or done anything that might question a teacher's authority. Betsy is never at home; Jana never leaves.

SELF-PUNISHING

A fragile but extremely pretty young woman, Sarah seems perfect on the outside. Her smooth face, blond hair, and straight white teeth are the status symbols so many other teens seem to want, but she knows she's not nearly as beautiful as her sister. In fact, in so many ways she feels inadequate. The skirt her mother bought just last week makes her look fat, although she's dropped 20 pounds in the last three months and is now down to 98. (Basically, food makes her sick and she wouldn't mind if she never ate again.) Even after studying as hard as she could, she could only get a B+ on her math test. Her father, the professor, only shook his head in pained dismay when he reviewed the test with her. She knows her mother is extremely disapproving of virtually any boy that seems interested in her. Even though Sarah is just a freshman, junior and senior boys have called her on the telephone. Sarah doesn't feel comfortable with them. The one boy she dated made fun of the way she walked and of the music station she selected on the car radio. The other girls call her "stuck up" and a snob, but she really isn't. She doesn't understand what is going on. "Why do I feel so alone?" she wonders. "Why can't I do

...ght? Why am I so unlovable?" Last night, ...t home alone watching late-night TV, she ...dered what it would feel like to take all those ...sthma pills in the bottle at once.

OBSESSIVELY COMPETITIVE

Gary appears to have more confidence than Kansas has grass, than Los Angeles has freeways. He says he never worries, because luck is surely on his side, but his competitive spirit is so obvious, he'll do just about anything to win. If the car in the next lane is going fast, he'll go faster, just to beat the other guy to the light. He's also ready to gamble, to challenge the odds. On poker night (or basketball or football night), you'll find no happier guy, because Gary loves the prospect of winning and taking your money, and usually has a little bet going on the side. Life kind of owes Gary, anyhow. So even when it looks like he might "lose," he does what he needs to do to make sure he doesn't get the short end of the stick. Take those stupid school exams, for instance. A busy guy like Gary can't always study, so what's the harm of taking the test out of the teacher's desk drawer the night before, photocopying it, and getting it back so no one is the wiser? Life is just a game anyway, we all know that, so why not do what you have to do to come out on top?

ANGRY

Darren has a lot of contempt for other people—especially adults, especially men. If an older guy were to ask Darren a simple question, like "Are you going to the game tonight?," Darren might say, "Why do you ask? Is it your business? Why shouldn't I go to the game if I want to?" Or he might throw a sneer, a sullen look, just to let the guy know he's less than dirt. Basically, Darren is always looking for a fight. Even when he's quietly not participating, not saying a word, he's provoking other

people by not giving them what they want, by not doing what they've asked him to do. Once put on the spot, Darren has so many good excuses; other people are nearly always to blame, and he's never responsible or at fault. You might say the world is Darren's battlefield. He assumes most people are going to try to control him, humiliate him by keeping him in their power. He'd like to show them! He's more powerful than anyone else, and he's ready to prove it by breaking the rules, breaking some windows, breaking a few legs.

FEARFUL

Gina blames herself for her younger brother's bad behavior. If Gina had only remembered to wait for him after school, Johnny wouldn't have thrown a tantrum at the bus stop and hit the little girl next door. It's so hard to do everything one is told to do. With her mom working, Gina has to care for her younger brothers and sisters after school, make dinner, do her homework, clean her room, and take care of her pet birds. On some days, the demands just seem overwhelming. When she tries to tell her mom she can't do everything, her mom gets so upset. Gina hates it when her mom cries or communicates her disapproval. When that happens, Gina clings to her stuffed animals in her tiny bedroom—the only space in the house where she feels safe. On the days when arguments between her mother and her mother's boyfriend escalate to shouting and throwing things, Gina feels most afraid. Things at school seem equally messed up. Actually, things are so bad she might as well run away. No one would really miss her—they'd only miss "the maid." Somewhere out there, there's got to be someone who will help her. She is 16 and can legally drop out of school, anyway. Some people think she looks 18. "Perhaps I can find an older friend," she thinks. "Like a handsome man who will really love me."

20 THINGS TO SAY OR DO FOR A FRIEND IN CRISIS

1. _____
2. _____
3. _____
4. _____
5. _____
6. _____
7. _____
8. _____
9. _____
10. _____
11. _____
12. _____
13. _____
14. _____
15. _____
16. _____
17. _____
18. _____
19. _____
20. _____

Remember:

It's ALWAYS okay to get help from trustworthy adults.

Getting help for yourself or a friend is NEVER a sign of weakness.

If this problem is getting out of hand, seek outside help TODAY.

LIFESKILLS

SESSION 5

THE EYE OF THE HURRICANE

Overview

With this session, the emphasis shifts from understanding what stress is all about to the description and practice of lifeskills. It begins by re-emphasizing the notion that we don't have to be victims of stress. We can learn different techniques and strategies that deal with stress both on an immediate basis (i.e., when there is a crisis at hand), but also in a proactive way (i.e., to keep ourselves from getting too stressed out in the first place).

The lifeskills introduced in the next eight sessions approach stress management from different angles or routes. Some techniques focus primarily on physical or mental strategies, others on interpersonal. Meditation is an example of a technique that combines physical and mental approaches simultaneously. In Session 1, the technique of progressive relaxation was introduced. In Session 5, we continue the theme of relaxing the body and centering the mind with meditation. Participants learn first about the theory and practice of meditation, and then engage in a preliminary exercise which focuses their attention on a simple task. After discussion of the experience, a second exercise in meditation is conducted. Westerners typically have great difficulty learning how to meditate, and the reasons for this are discussed in closing the session.

Overall Goals Relevant to This Session

After completing this session, participants should:

Know the difference between a state of stress and relaxed well-being.

Experience the benefits of a range of lifeskills: physical activity, relaxation, assertiveness, supportive relationships, life planning, and positive "self-talk."

Learner Outcomes

The purpose of this session is to help teens to:

1. Understand how the mind can influence the stress a body feels.

2. Learn what it means to slow time down and increase their awareness of the present.

3. Experience the calm that comes from centering the mind.

4. Understand some of the societal messages which may inhibit their openness to meditation.

Relevant Chapters in the Student Book

■ Part III, "Taking Care of #1," the section entitled "Finding the Eye of the Hurricane" (pp. 70–82)

Agenda

In order to accomplish these outcomes, leaders need to:

1. Present a mini-lecture on the purpose and art of meditation (10 minutes).

2. Lead teens through a preliminary exercise in which they learn how to increasingly focus their attention on a simple task (15 minutes).

3. Conduct a meditation exercise (15 minutes).

4. Discuss the cultural influences that inhibit Westerners from using this approach to stress management (10 minutes).

Resources and Materials

- "Script for Centering Attention on a Simple Task" (pages 63–64)

- "Meditation Script" (page 65)

- Bag of M & M candies

- Stopwatch or clock with a second hand

- Quiet room

- Handout of "Relaxation Audiotape Project" (page 121) (optional)

Activities

1. Present a mini-lecture on the purpose and art of meditation.

Begin by preparing the group to make the transition from thinking about stressors, stress reactions, and inappropriate coping strategies, to the concept that we don't have to be victims to stress. We don't have to be passive. We can learn new techniques for managing stress both on a physical and mental level. Today's session introduces a very healthy and positive strategy: meditation. Like other relaxation exercises, meditation is a structured way to let go of worries and tension. To make sure that participants understand what relaxation is, ask them to explain the difference between a quiet activity, such as reading a book or watching television, and the kind of relaxation done in yoga (e.g., the "sponge" position), or in meditation. Clarify that relaxation is a form of "non-doing," "focused rest," "passive attention," "centering." There are many different kinds of relaxation techniques. Ask teens if they can recall from their reading three characteristics that relaxation techniques have in common. As listed on page 71 of the student book, relaxation techniques:

- must be learned, and they must be practiced

- induce noticeable, measurable physiological changes

- involve a neutral focus of attention (rather than thinking).

Relaxation techniques require disciplined learning and practice because it is not easy to screen out the steady thought processes of the mind, nor is it simple to quiet a tense body.

In our culture, progressive relaxation and meditation are increasingly being considered positive by many people, including members of the medical establishment (see Bill Moyers's book, *Healing and the Mind,* for examples). These strategies are known to help people endure acute anxiety (such as test anxiety, or fear of the dentist's chair) and acute pain (such as natural childbirth). In other cultures, meditation and relaxation exercises play a major part in people's daily lives; for them, such exercises become proactive lifeskills.

Both progressive relaxation and meditation produce similar physical responses in the body. In the early 1960s, these physiological changes were studied by Dr. Herbert Benson at Harvard Medical School. Because of these studies, Benson hypothesized that the relaxation response is the opposite of the fight-or-flight response.[1] Specifically, Benson found that during relaxation, oxygen consumption decreases by 13%, carbon dioxide production decreases by 12%, and eleven to sixteen fewer breaths are taken per minute. He also found a correlation between regular relaxation, relatively low blood pressures, decreased heart rates, decreased blood lactate (a waste product of metabolism), and the intensification of Alpha brain waves. Benson continues to find that regular application of relaxation techniques makes people less susceptible to stressors. More noradrenaline (the "stress chemical" in the brain) is actually required to cause a rise in blood pressure and heart rate in people who relax regularly than in the person who never plans purposeful relaxation. Today, Benson has developed a four-part instructional series on the relaxation response that draws on different historical uses of meditation and relaxation techniques.

Meditation has been a mainstay of both Eastern and Western religious leaders for centuries. In meditation, the body is relaxed (usually in a sitting position), and attention is focused on a neutral visual object (e.g., a blank wall) or sound (e.g., chanting). The mind is alert but detached from intellectual activity. Although meditation is imbued with rich religious traditions, its primary benefits to some may be in the psychophysical changes it causes. As Katsuki Sekida explains, "Zen is not in my view a philosophy or mysticism. It is simply a practice of readjustment of nervous activity. That is, it restores the distorted nervous system to its normal functioning."[2]

In answer to the question, "What exactly is meditation?," one answer is that it is "a way of looking deeply into the chatter of the mind and body and becoming more aware of its patterns. By observing it, you free yourself from much of it. And then the chatter will calm down."[3] Similarly, "Meditation is a discipline for training the mind to develop greater calm and then to use that calm to bring penetrative insight into our own experience in the moment."[4] By learning to calm the mind and body, people often experience enhanced physical and spiritual well-being.

2. Lead teens through a preliminary exercise in which they learn how to increasingly focus their attention on a simple task.

In order to prepare teens for meditation, a preliminary exercise should be done to calm them down and begin thinking about centering on the present moment. Use the "Script for Centering Attention on a Simple Task" on pages 63–64, or develop your own variations.

3. Conduct a meditation exercise.

Now explain to participants that they are ready to try a brief meditation exercise. Meditation techniques vary, but they generally involve focusing on a particular sound (e.g., "Om"), or name, or number, and its repetition. To do the meditation exercise, give teens instructions on how to assume the training position and then proceed (see the "Meditation Script" on page 65). For this session, students should only be expected to meditate for a period of ten minutes. The remainder of the allotted time is spent setting up and discussing the experience with the students.

4. Discuss the cultural influences that inhibit Westerners from using this approach to stress management.

Common difficulties for first-time meditators include itchy, twitchy bodies and restless minds, feeling silly, losing track of time, forgetting which number they're on, bodily aches and discomfort—even loneliness.

Help teens understand that this is the restless part of them that resists slowing down. It requires patience and practice to slow the steady stream of activity in one's mind and body. Have students talk about some of the things that interfered with their ability to concentrate, to relax. (Have them also talk about the positive outcomes.)

If your participants did not experience the anticipated benefits of meditation this first time, encourage them to try it again at home or with a friend. It takes a lot of practice and a long time before people acquire this skill. You might want to ask participants to reflect on how we are taught to "relax" in this culture. For example:

- Is it okay to sit alone in a quiet room, not watching television or reading a book, not doing anything in particular? Why or why not? How does it feel to do that?

- It is okay to go for a walk, without a destination or goal in mind?

- What do you or your family do for vacations? How much actual time is spent relaxing and letting the time unfold, as opposed to programming yourself with non-stop activity? What is the most relaxing part of the vacation?

- Are Americans prone to medicating themselves with various drugs (e.g., sedatives, alcohol, muscle relaxers) to calm down? Why do you think they are, or aren't?

- If there are students with Asian or Indian heritage in your group, ask them to describe what their parents or culture have taught them about relaxation.

Summarize the session by reviewing the benefits of relaxation. As suggested on page 82 of the student book, relaxation skills are important because they:

- help people feel less crazy, worried, and insecure

- help people get control of their minds and bodies

- give the body a chance to recover from the stress of everyday life

- can provide enormous amounts of new energy, both physical and mental

- help people feel good about themselves and about life.

Suggestions for Other Activities and Projects

■ One ideal project for youth groups is the making of their own relaxation audiotape. See "Relaxation Audiotape Project" (page 121) for a handout explaining this project.

■ Have students develop their own centering and meditation scripts.

■ Bring in a guest teacher (e.g., yoga instructor or other relaxation educator) to demonstrate a relaxation technique.

■ It may help to have some slides or visuals of different relaxation postures and activities to show, either up on the wall or ready to pass around the room—perhaps posters of different yoga classes or yogis from India, or slides of Buddhist monks in temple, meditating. You may also wish to show videotapes of how relaxation exercises are performed. Local hospitals may have teaching tapes that demonstrate deep breathing techniques for women in childbirth classes. Also, a regional chapter of CEA (Childbirth Education Association) may have tapes to lend. In addition, check with a medical school library if one is nearby; it might have a videotape that demonstrates how progressive relaxation techniques or biofeedback are used in physical therapy. Visuals are particularly helpful in this session, both to create a mood and give students a picture of the activities they're practicing.

REFERENCES

1. Restak, R. The Brain. (New York: Bantam Books, 1984), pp. 177–178.
2. Ibid., p. 181.
3. Moyers, Bill. *Healing and the Mind*. (New York: Doubleday, 1993), p. 126.
4. Ibid., p. 127.
5. Ibid., p. 127.

SCRIPT FOR CENTERING ATTENTION ON A SIMPLE TASK

"Much of the time we run around so much on automatic pilot, and we have so much chatter going on, and we're so busy, we hardly know who's doing the doing. Meditation is a way of slowing down enough so that we get in touch with who we are, and then we can inform the doing with a greater level of awareness and consciousness."[5]

—Jon Kabat-Zinn, "Healing from Within," in Bill Moyers, *Healing and the Mind*

LOOSENING UP THE BODY

Before we begin the meditation exercise, we're going to do a few things. First, we're all going to stand up and stretch our hands up high in the air, inhaling a great big breath as we go, and then we're going to bend over and let our hands dangle down toward our feet (only as far as it is comfortable), exhaling as we do so. Okay, now just rest there for a moment, close your eyes, and continue to breath slowly and deeply. Now slowly roll up, beginning with your lower back, and inching up along your spine, keeping your head down until the very last. When your head comes up, take another good breath. Okay, now we're going to repeat the process. *(Repeat.)*

EATING THE FIRST M & M

(Pass out the M & Ms so each person has five.) I want you now to pick up one M & M and eat it. I'm going to time you with this stopwatch. Everybody ready? Okay, go ahead and do it...now!

All done? Okay, that took approximately 1.5 seconds. Somebody tell me how the candy tasted. What color was it, by the way? Was it good? Was it very satisfying?

EATING THE SECOND M & M

Okay, in a moment we're going to eat another M & M, but before you do, I want you to think about eating this one slowly. I want you to think about what the candy really tastes like by letting it sit in your mouth for a while and chewing it as slowly as possible. Become as focused as you can on this one piece of candy, and this one piece of candy alone. Try to be as aware as you can of everything about this one M & M. How does it feel going down your throat? How does it feel in your stomach? I will time you again with the stopwatch. Let me know when you are completely done with eating this candy by raising your hand.

(When the group is ready....)

Okay, that took (X number of seconds). Somebody tell me now what they noticed about the candy this time around that they didn't notice the first time. Did the candy taste better, or different? What was the experience like? Was the eating experience more pleasurable? Is there more of an aftertaste?

EATING THE THIRD M & M

As you can probably guess, we're going to do this again. This time I'm going to tell you to slow down the process of eating even more. This time, I want you to look at the M & M before you eat it, and notice everything you can about its appearance. How big is it? What is its shape, color, texture? Think about nothing but this one M & M. Concentrate on what it tastes like and how it feels in your mouth. Once it is in your mouth, see if you can really feel its different parts as well as taste it. Last time, it took most of you (X number of seconds) to eat this M & M. Let's see if you can spend twice that number of seconds this time around.

(Proceed with the exercise. When the group is done, comment on the increase—or decrease—in time).

Did you discover anything new about the candy? What was the experience like? Was the candy as good, or better? Or did your mind start to wander? What did you think about, if you stopped thinking about the candy? Did you start to have parallel thoughts—that is, thoughts about the candy, and thoughts about yourself eating the candy?

EATING THE FOURTH M & M

We're going to do this activity again for the last time, and this time I want you to close your eyes. I want you to focus on nothing but yourself, as you hold on to the M & M and put it in your mouth. See if you can "see" the whole event from beginning to end, and experience everything about the eating of this M & M that there is to experience. Make it a complete, seamless activity, as though every part of it had tremendous meaning. Proceed at your own pace.

(When the group is done....)

Okay, that was interesting; as a group, you generally spent a (longer or shorter) amount of time eating the candy compared to the previous time. Why do you suppose that is? What happened? Did you notice anything new about the candy? Could you see yourself eating the M & M? Now, quickly scan your body state; how are you feeling? Do you feel relaxed? Do you feel kind of curious, but calm?

This activity was a simple way to introduce the notion to you that we often go through life by not paying much attention to it. We're doing so many different things simultaneously, we have to block out our awareness. Life can actually seem to have more richness—food can taste more delicious, breathing can feel more invigorating—if we slow down and concentrate on what we are doing. When we do this, we may find our bodies relaxing as our minds become more focused.

EATING THE FIFTH M & M

You may eat the fifth M & M any way you want to.

MEDITATION SCRIPT

Everyone please find a firm chair and turn it toward a blank portion of the wall. Sit as far apart from the next person as possible. Sit facing the wall with your back relaxed but straight. Your feet should be flat on the floor. Fold your hands in your lap or lay them along the tops of your thighs. Keeping your head upright, tuck your chin back and in. Keep your eyes open and look down at about a 45-degree angle. You should be staring at the wall directly in front of you. The purpose here is to align your body so it feels balanced and strong. This position may seem tiring at first, but over time it is easier because spinal alignment allows the back muscles to be more relaxed. It also allows the diaphragm to expand more fully when breathing, which helps calm and slow the body.

This is the basic training posture. When you assume it, you join a company of meditators all over the world. To do this meditation exercise, maintain this posture in silence and count your breaths. Please breathe through your nose as we learned to do in the previous relaxation exercises. You'll inhale and silently count "one," then exhale and silently count "two," and so on up to "ten."

When you reach "ten," start over again on "one" with the next inhalation. Think of yourself as "riding the waves" of your breath, just as a rubber raft goes up and down on a gentle ocean swell. The only thing you have to do is "go with the flow."

Here are some guidelines for first-time meditators:

1. Don't try to manipulate your breathing, just let it come naturally. Your body knows how to breathe. Let your body do what it knows how to do.

2. Keep your body still. A restless body creates a restless mind.

3. Keep counting and keep focused until I tell you it's time to stop.

4. If your mind wanders, gently bring it back to the number "one" and start counting again, along with the breath.

5. Don't worry about doing it "wrong." That's just a thought—a distraction. Go back to "one" and start counting again.

GETTING PHYSICAL

Overview

Perhaps the most basic, fundamental lifeskill is that of maintaining our physical health. Eating sensibly, getting enough sleep, not smoking, avoiding transmittable diseases (and all those other things your mother told you about!) are all part of staying healthy. Additionally, maintaining our body's fitness and stamina are crucial lifeskills that help us manage stress over the long haul.

In Sessions 1 and 5, progressive relaxation and other exercises were introduced. Knowing how to deeply relax is part of the challenge to physical fitness: the other part requires active engagement, or actual physical activity. Physical activity differs from competitive sports and (some) exercise routines, both of which can build bodies, but can also create terrific mental, physical, and emotional strain. When approached with the right mind set, physical activity can be a very effective way to release stored tension and improve the body's overall machinery. A healthy body handles the psychophysical demands of stress more effectively. It also burns fat; improves circulation, lung capacity, and muscle tone; and maintains overall physical health and strength.

In this session, teens learn the basic principles of aerobic exercise and participate in an activity in which their target heart rates are determined. They also generate appropriate and unique activity prescriptions for themselves. Additional activities include a "Teen Inventory on Physical Activity." For those participants interested in contracting with the leader or a friend (or other adult) for long-term change, a "Lifeskill Contract" is available (see pages 122–123).

Overall Goal Relevant to This Session

After completing this session, participants should:

Experience the benefits of a range of lifeskills: physical activity, relaxation, assertiveness, supportive relationships, life planning, and positive "self-talk."

Learner Outcomes

The purpose of this session is to help teens to:

1. Identify the cultural norms surrounding physical activity.

2. Distinguish between relaxation (i.e., the body during a resting state) and physical activity (i.e., the body at a training rate of activity).

3. Generate their own personal activity prescription that takes into account appropriate intensity, duration, and frequency.

Relevant Chapters in the Student Book

■ Part III, "Taking Care of #1," the section entitled "Use It or Lose It" (pp. 56–61)

Agenda

In order to accomplish these outcomes, leaders need to:

1. Discuss the cultural norms surrounding physical activity (15 minutes).

2. Conduct an aerobic exercise in which students determine their resting, maximum, and target heart rates (15 minutes).

3. Demonstrate how to apply the FIT formula (20 minutes).

Resources and Materials

- "Script for Determining Target Heart Rates" (page 70)

- Handout of "Target Heart Rate Worksheet" (page 71)

- Handout or overhead of "Physical Activities That Can Reduce Stress" (page 72)

- A large, mostly empty classroom or gym with floor mats

- Stopwatch or clock with second hand

- Jump ropes (single person ropes)

- Record or tape of music with steady, moderate beat (optional)

- Overhead projector and screen (optional)

- Handout of "Teen Inventory on Physical Activity" (pages 73–74) (optional)

- Handout of "Lifeskill Contract" (pages 122–123) (optional)

Activities

1. Discuss the cultural norms surrounding physical activity.

Begin the session by saying that one extremely important component of stress management is keeping oneself physically fit. When we are children, this seems ridiculously easy, because we spend so much time in physical play. As we mature, powerful cultural norms begin to shape our feelings about our bodies and our willingness to establish physical routines. As bodies slow down naturally with age, the temptation to become more and more sedentary increases. It is easier to "keep using it" than starting up again, once one has "lost it." But it is never too late to decide to be more physically fit, and something can always be gained from doing so, even when the effort is modest.

When improving one's physical conditioning, it helps to have reinforcement and support from others. Generally, the more difficult the behavior change, the greater the need for such support and reinforcement. Although the concept of physical fitness has become more diverse and more acceptable in the last decade, the "movement" seems to have taken greatest hold with professionals in the 20-to-40-year-old range; there are still a lot of teens who drop out of sports, never learn to dance, and stop exercising their bodies by the time they are 16. Ask participants to join you in thinking about the reasons why it may be hard for some teens to keep themselves physically active in this culture. Ask what "messages" they have picked up around school, home, or the media about:

- Who should play games? Who should play competitive sports?

- What are the options if you don't want to play competitive sports?

- What does a healthy body look like for women/girls?

- What does a healthy body look like for men/boys?

- What's so "good" about being physically fit? What's the point of doing it?

- What do you need to have or do to stay physically fit?

- How hard should you work out to get fit? Is the process supposed to be pleasant or painful?

Some responses that may emerge from this discussion are that "only kids play games" and "only athletically talented and competitive should play sports." Many traditional group opportunities for physical movement (e.g., folk dance, figure skating in the park, tobogganing) no longer exist, or are considered "nerdy" by sophisticated teens. Women and girls are held to an impossibly thin and unhealthy body image; men and boys over-rate muscular development and sheer height or size as synonymous with fitness.

What keeps teens from engaging in activity? To some extent, it is lack of imagination (many young people don't know how to "play" anymore, they are so conditioned to being entertained). To some extent, it

67

is the result of aggressive marketing of sporting goods companies, and the idea that you need hundreds of dollars of the "right" equipment and the "right" clothes before you can set foot out the door. And, realistically, there is a certain amount of discipline involved. For teens who are into spontaneous "fun," the whole business may seem basically grim, painful, and a whole lot of work.

2. Conduct an exercise to determine resting, maximum, and target heart rates.

Explain that aerobics is just one form of physical activity, but that it serves as a good illustration of how physical movement can release stored tension and be healthful in other ways. Aerobic exercise is steady exercise that demands an uninterrupted output from your muscles over a 20–30 minute period. An increase in heart rate during physical activity is an indirect measure of how hard the muscles are working. The main criterion for aerobics, then, is continuous and steady activity that maintains a person's heart rate at the proper target rate. As the body exercises aerobically, lung capacity and circulation are improved, as is the body's overall physical condition.

Any number of physical activities can reduce stored tension, which is good for stress management. Recall that the fight-or-flight response prepares the body for action. Even if a person doesn't engage in any action, the body still goes through the chain of events in preparation to fight or flee. The physical results of unreleased tension are restlessness, anxiety, and physical tension. Unreleased tension gets expressed by constantly tapping one's fingers or toes or other constant motion, or by the urgent feelings, "I've got to get out of here!" "I've got to get going!" This energy is physical/chemical in nature and needs release.

Although strenuous physical activity can cause injuries and general wear and tear, a moderate amount releases tension and creates a degree of relaxation. One way to determine the right kind and amount of physical activity for yourself is the FIT formula, which is described on pages 58–61 of the student book. This formula operates on aerobic principles. Participants can experience this approach as you lead them through the "Script for Determining Target Heart Rates" (page 70).

When the activity is over, explain that what teens just experienced was the physical difference between their body's *resting state* and an *active state* which represents approximately 60–70% of their maximum heart rate. Pulse level indicates stress, as they've learned through the fight-or-flight response. The *maximum heart rate* equals too much stress (it could be lethal, especially when they are older) and is not considered a good pace for any sport or exercise. The *target heart rate* identifies a comfortable level of exercise (stress) for achieving aerobic conditioning. *Working harder than this rate doesn't greatly increase the benefit gained from the activity.*

It is important to respect individual differences in physical conditioning and capability, and to encourage participants to respect themselves and each other in this regard. When you conduct or lead the aerobic exercise, make sure you look out for participants who are overweight, have a physical handicap or disability, or have any other condition which may make the exercise difficult or inappropriate. Watch how you partner kids together. Teens will naturally try to keep up with each other, but one partner's pace may be too intense for the other. Some very fit kids may need to exercise twice as hard as others to get their heart rate up to the target level. Others may raise it sufficiently just by walking vigorously. Make sure you counsel participants to choose an activity that feels comfortable and can be sustained for five minutes. If they can't talk to each other, or whistle or sing (softly) while doing the exercise, they're probably working too hard.

3. Demonstrate how to apply the FIT formula.

Pass around the handout (or show the overhead) "Physical Activities That Can Reduce Stress" (page 72). Share with teens (our) philosophy that we needn't be superstars to enjoy and use our bodies. The trick is to find the right activity (or variety of activities), the right **F**requency, the right **I**ntensity level, and the right amount of **T**ime (**FIT**) for the activity.

Ask a volunteer to select an interesting-sounding activity from among those listed on the handout. Problem-solve with that person how he or she might reasonably engage in that activity in ways that would release tension and promote fitness. For example, if the individual likes to ride a bike, then riding a bike for about a half hour, three times a week, maintaining a steady rate without getting short of breath, is an appropriate activity prescription for him or her. Repeat the FIT formula process with one or two other participants. (This exercise could be given as an individual assignment.)

Ask teens to identify the successful activities they already use, as well as any obstacles they encounter when trying to use physical activity routinely as a stress reducer. Is it their own lack of interest? Cost of equipment? Lack of a friend to do it with? Lack of time, or other obligations? Problem-solve a couple of these obstacles. Suggest some ways people might creatively choose or alter an activity, combine it with another task, or schedule it with a friend. Examples are:

- Power-walk the mall before shopping.

- Join a water ballet class rather than speed swimming.

- Do a different aerobic activity each week to prevent boredom.

- Make a 20-minute tape of favorite music and dance every afternoon after school.

- Roller blade your way to the library and back.

- Play co-ed soccer for fun, and don't keep score.

- Play any mixed-age team sports (e.g., soccer, volleyball) and don't keep score.

- Take Tai Chi classes as a way to learn about another culture.

End the session with the viewpoint that finding ways to become more physically active can become kind of a fun challenge.

Suggestions for Other Activities and Projects

- Invite the physical education or local aerobics teacher to co-teach this session if you prefer not to lead the aerobic exercise yourself. Choose some lively music to accompany the exercise to make the atmosphere fun.

- To extend or amplify this session, consider using the "Teen Inventory on Physical Activity" (pages 73–74) as a preliminary exercise before discussing cultural norms. If your setting accommodates long-term projects, consider having students construct a "Lifeskill Contract" (see pages 122–123).

Recommended Reading

- Bailey, C. *The New Fit or Fat.* (Boston: Houghton Mifflin Company, 1991.)

SCRIPT FOR DETERMINING TARGET HEART RATES

As you provide the instructions below, circulate the "Target Heart Rate Worksheet" (page 71).

First, we're going to determine your *resting heart rate* by taking your pulse for ten seconds. To find your pulse, place your index and middle fingers (not thumb) either on your wrist near the thumb, or on your neck alongside of the Adam's apple. Everyone have it? Okay, you're going to count the number of beats while I time you. Starting counting…now! *(Ten seconds later):* Okay, stop! How many beats did you get? Let's do it one more time and get it as exact as you can. Multiply that number by six and record it on your worksheet under "Resting Heart Rate."

Next, to calculate your *maximum heart rate*, subtract your age from 220, then list the difference on the worksheet. Good! Finally, to find your target heart rate, look on the table on your worksheet. Find your maximum heart rate on one of the rows going down the left-hand side of the table, and your resting heart rate among the column headers at the top. Your target heart rate is in the square that matches this row and column. This number represents the maximum beats per minute for the most beneficial workout.

Now we're going to bring your heart up to this target rate. First, choose an activity—either jumping rope, power walking, jogging, or dancing—and find a partner who's interested in doing the same activity. When I say "begin," start doing the activity together, but talk to each other while you do your activity. *If you can't keep up a conversation, slow down the activity: you're working too hard.*

Make sure your partner doesn't overdo it! Quite likely, the two of you will have different target rates, and your will reach your target rates at different paces. We'll do this activity for a minute or two, then stop to see whether your pulse is within ten points of your target rate. We'll do that by again taking your pulse for ten seconds and multiplying that answer by six. You must *stop* when I say "stop" and time yourself, because your heart will begin to "recover" (slow down) almost immediately.

TARGET HEART RATE WORKSHEET

Resting Heart Rate

To calculate your resting heart rate, take your pulse for exactly ten seconds and multiply your answer by six.

Resting Heart Rate = _____

Maximum Heart Rate

To determine your maximum heart rate, subtract your age from 220.

Maximum Heart Rate = _____

Target Heart Rate

To determine your target heart rate, look at the table below. Locate your maximum heart rate in the column at the left side of the table, and your resting heart rate in the row of column headers at the top. Your target rate (beats per minute) is listed where the row and column meet.

Target Heart Rate = _____

RESTING HEART RATE

(Numbers have been rounded off to nearest .50)

		50	55	60	65	70
	210	186.5	191.5	196.5	201.5	206.5
MAXIMUM	**209**	185	191	196	200	206
HEART	**208**	185	190	195	200	205
RATE	**207**	184.5	189.5	194.5	199.5	204.5
	206	184	189	194	199	204
	205	183	188	193	198	203
	204	182.5	187.5	192.5	197.5	202.5
	203	182	187	192	197	202

More important than the actual number is how you feel while doing your activity. Getting fit doesn't have to be uncomfortable. If you are out of breath or feel discomfort, you are overdoing it.

PHYSICAL ACTIVITIES THAT CAN REDUCE STRESS

Gymnastics	Throwing a Frisbee	Rowing
Roller Blading	Ice Skating	Surfing
Swimming	Kayaking	Tennis
Bowling	Boxing	Jogging
Golf	Bicycling	Basketball
Football	Jumping Rope	Skiing
Lacrosse	Baseball	Ice Hockey
Wood Chopping	Wrestling	Weightlifting
Dancing	Handball	Racquetball
Squash	Badminton	Ping Pong
Volleyball	Croquet	Isometrics
Power Walking	Juggling	Softball
Hiking	Tai Chi	Yoga
Martial Arts	Canoeing	Horseback Riding
Skateboarding	Mime	Field Hockey
Track and Field	Snow Shoeing	Soccer

Some of these activities are much better stress-reducers than others. Can you explain why? Which might work best for you? How could you make more of these activities fun and relaxing for you?

Apply the FIT formula to your preferred activities.

The FIT Formula

Frequency	=	3 sessions per week
Intensity	=	at or close to your target heart rate
Time	=	20–30 minutes per session

From *A Leader's Guide to Fighting Invisible Tigers* by Connie C. Schmitz, Ph.D., with Earl Hipp, copyright © 1995. Free Spirit Publishing Inc, Minneapolis, MN; 866/703-7322; www.freespirit.com. This page may be photocopied for individual classroom or small group work only.

TEEN INVENTORY ON PHYSICAL ACTIVITY

The purpose of this inventory is to help you start thinking about your attitudes and previous history with physical activities.

1 The words "physical exercise" and "sports" conjure up different emotions for different people. To some teens, for example, physical education is the best (and perhaps only) good thing about school. They simply *have* to move around; sitting still is torture. To others, physical education is the worst part of their day. Everything remotely related to sports and exercise is frustrating, boring, or embarrassing. Too often, kids and adults live in the shadow of athletes with heroic status; we feel compelled to compete at their level or sit on the sidelines. Think about what sports and physical activities in general have meant for you. Have they been important? How so? Why or why not? *Write your ideas down briefly below.*

_____

_____

_____

_____

_____

2 If you have negative feelings about physical activities, can you remember how it felt to move around and play in a physical way when you were younger? Do you have any positive memories of playing, riding bikes, sliding down hills? If so, what were these activities, and why were they enjoyable?

_____

_____

_____

_____

3 Which kinds of physical activities seem to work the best for you? Which give you the most pleasure or fun? Why? Which kinds of activities do you enjoy doing the least? Why don't you enjoy them?

_____

_____

_____

_____

_____

➡

Teen Inventory on Physical Activity continued

4 Is physical activity a regular part of your day? Explain why or why not, and how (if applicable).

_____

_____

_____

_____

_____

5 How would you describe your overall physical condition? Do you feel good about your body in terms of energy, stamina, strength?

_____

_____

_____

_____

_____

6 Most of the chronic health problems in America today are related to lifestyle, and that includes lack of exercise. Physical activity doesn't have to be competitive or dreary. Use the information you've gained about yourself here to write a short activity prescription using the FIT formula.

_____

_____

_____

_____

_____

The FIT Formula

Frequency	=	3 sessions per week
Intensity	=	at or close to your target heart rate
Time	=	20–30 minutes per session

From *A Leader's Guide to Fighting Invisible Tigers* by Connie C. Schmitz, Ph.D., with Earl Hipp, copyright © 1995. Free Spirit Publishing Inc, Minneapolis, MN; 866/703-7322; *www.freespirit.com*. This page may be photocopied for individual classroom or small group work only.

SESSION 7

COMMUNICATION STYLES

Overview

As we saw in Sessions 1, 5, and 6, relaxation and physical activity are important lifeskills because they release tension, focus the mind, and build stamina. By comparison, communication skills deal with the psychological stress of human relations. Teenagers invest a tremendous amount of time and emotional energy adjusting to their new peer culture, which is so suddenly and radically different than childhood. Subsequently, they spend a lot of time worrying about interpersonal relationships—mostly about their relations with girlfriends, boyfriends, and other friends, but also about their relations with parents, siblings, and other adults. Simply communicating their own needs, thoughts, and opinions (both positive and negative) can be stressful for teens. Failing to communicate, or communicating poorly, can also lead to problems. By learning how to assert themselves verbally in various situations, teens can alleviate interpersonal conflicts and strengthen relationships.

In this session, participants start to look at the effects of communication styles on relationships. They define assertiveness and learn about passive, aggressive, passive-aggressive, and assertive communication styles.

Overall Goal Relevant to This Session

After completing this session, participants should:

Experience the benefits of a range of lifeskills: physical activity, relaxation, assertiveness, supportive relationships, life planning, and positive "self-talk."

Learner Outcomes

The purpose of this session is to help teens to:

1. Define passive, aggressive, passive-aggressive, and assertive styles of communication.

2. Explain the needs and motivations behind each type of response style, as well as the consequences of each style.

3. Identify some of the cultural norms and stereotypes surrounding these behaviors.

4. Identify the benefits of being assertive.

Relevant Chapters in the Student Book

■ Part III, "Being Assertive" (pp. 83–99)

Agenda

In order to accomplish these outcomes, leaders need to:

1. Describe passive, aggressive, passive-aggressive, and assertive behavior styles (15 minutes).

2. Conduct a small group exercise in which students identify and discuss these behaviors, as described in written scenarios (20 minutes).

3. Summarize discussion by listing the motivations and cultural norms surrounding each communication style (15 minutes).

Resources and Materials

- Handout of "Response Styles Worksheet" (pages 80–81)

- Handout of "Teen Inventory on Communication Styles" (pages 82–83) (optional)

- Chalkboard or easel pad

Activities

1. Describe four communication response styles.

Begin by explaining that communication can be considered one of the most important of all lifeskills because it does something directly about the source of interpersonal stress. The way we talk to each other—our friends, relatives, teachers—can either pull people forward or push them away; it can either create conflict, resentment, and confusion, or engender trust, liking, and cooperation. Assertive communication is a particular style of communication that can help people feel less like victims and more in control of their lives. Assertive communication enables a person to protect his or her basic rights while respecting the rights of others. An assertive interpersonal style also leads to more honest, enjoyable, and long-lasting relationships. In short, developing assertive communication skills can prevent stress and promote self-respect and intimacy with others.

Concepts of assertiveness can be traced back to psychologists working in the 1940s, but assertiveness skills weren't systematically defined or taught until the 1970s, when assertiveness training became popular. Ask if students can define assertiveness. We favor a definition supplied by Robert Alberti and Michael Emmons:

> *"Assertive behavior enables a person to act in his or her own best interest, to stand up for herself or himself without undue anxiety, to express honest feelings comfortably, or to exercise personal rights without denying the rights of others."*[1]

> **— Robert Alberti and Michael Emmons,**
> ***Your Perfect Right***

THE ASSERTIVE RESPONSE STYLE

Building on the definition above, have participants give examples of situations in which people "act in their own best interests," "stand up for themselves," "express their feelings honestly," and "exercise their personal rights without denying the rights of others." Don't rush through this definition, as it's important that everyone understand just what kinds of behavior are implied. Of the many examples that could be cited, here are a few:

- Acting in one's own best interests:
  - Talking to a teacher when confused
  - When home with a cold, asking a friend for the homework assignment
  - Training hard before a team try-out or marathon
  - Deciding which colleges you (not your parents) want to apply to
  - Deciding to organize a party or school event.

- Standing up for oneself:
  - Saying "no" to uncomfortable social invitations (e.g., drinking beer or accepting a ride with someone you don't know)
  - Defending a personal decision, action, or belief
  - Responding to criticism
  - Explaining an answer to a (teacher's) question more thoroughly.

- Expressing feelings:
  - Honestly and respectfully disagreeing with a friend
  - Thanking a parent or sibling for his or her help
  - Telling someone you're afraid, worried, or angry
  - Saying "You're great!" or "I like you!"

- Exercising one's personal rights:
  - Expressing a political viewpoint
  - Confronting a teacher, parent, or coach about a problem

- Returning defective merchandise
- Asking other people not to smoke in a no-smoking area
- Asking for feedback or explanations from others.
- Respecting the rights of others
  - Choosing not to call other people names
  - Choosing not to threaten, bribe, or manipulate other people
  - Choosing not to hurt other people (physically, emotionally)
  - Choosing not to lie about people or events in order to gain control
  - Respecting each person's independent viewpoint, decisions, needs, differences.

Contrast the assertive response style with the passive, aggressive, and passive-aggressive response styles.

THE PASSIVE RESPONSE STYLE

A person operating with a passive response style allows other people to make all the decisions, to control his or her feelings or actions. Overly passive people may not even be aware of having strong feelings or opinions. Because they don't believe their thoughts or feelings "count," they deny their own needs, or consistently put them last, and work very hard to please other people. This often leaves passive people feeling hurt, anxious, angry, let down, and depressed because they can't get their own needs met. Passive people may also feel lonely, as they are without true friends—i.e., friends who don't "use" them.

THE AGGRESSIVE RESPONSE STYLE

A person operating with an aggressive response style is apt to be loud, abusive, "pushy," and sarcastic. Examples of an aggressive style include people who: gossip maliciously; boss, tease, or humiliate other people in public; physically threaten others; need to win every argument; or control other people's decisions or feelings. Achieving a personal goal at the expense of others is not a problem for the aggressive person. By definition, his or her own needs come first. While an aggressive style makes people feel

powerful on the surface, it costs them a lot in terms of trust and respect. It, too, leaves the person with few close friends and many unmet needs.

THE PASSIVE-AGGRESSIVE RESPONSE STYLE

People who operate with a passive-aggressive response style combine elements of the two preceding styles. They do not overtly dominate or abuse other people, but seek control or revenge covertly (sometimes unconsciously) instead. Passive-aggressive people, for example, say "yes" with an insincere smile and never follow through. They are persistently late; their commitments aren't solid. They keep quiet when an unfair or difficult decision is being made, then quietly sabotage it behind the scenes. Although passive-aggressive people are angry, they don't know how to directly express their anger, and they fear the anger or disapproval of people who have power or are "in charge." Like passive people, they see themselves as victims who can't change oppressive (or even benign) circumstances. Like aggressive people, their methods for gaining power disrespects the rights and feelings of others.

RECOGNIZING COMMUNICATION STYLES

Explain to teens that we all have used passive, aggressive, and passive-aggressive styles of communication at different times in our lives. We're human beings, we're imperfect, so at times we do fail to speak up, or we speak out in anger in an abusive way, or we quietly seek revenge. One hopes we use some assertive behaviors as well.

Make sure it's clear that the examples above illustrate people who consistently operate out of one mode and are exaggerations of how most people interact. When going over these definitions, bring participants into the discussion by asking them to provide examples of different response styles, and to compare them.

2. Conduct a small group exercise.

Have teens form small groups and pass around the "Response Styles Worksheet" (pages 80–81). For each of the vignettes, have them identify the four different communication styles and to think about the motivations of each of the characters in the scene. Tell them to discuss the imagined consequences of each behavior style. Then ask students to figure out how the situations could be handled differently by an assertive person.

3. Discuss the motivations and cultural norms surrounding each communication style.

To summarize the small group activity (and the session), ask teens why they think the characters described in the written scenarios used the response style they did. Why did they respond aggressively, or assertively, or passively, or with a passive-aggressive style? List these reasons on the chalkboard and elaborate on them with the suggestions given below:

- Why are some people passive? Because...

  - They don't know how to be assertive.

  - They fear the loss of approval and support from others.

  - They want to avoid conflict and keep the peace.

  - Feeling like a victim is all they know.

  - They mistake assertiveness for aggressiveness.

  - They mistake passivity for femininity or "being good."

  - They are uncertain about their basic rights.

  - They get a lot of rewards for being passive.

  - They fear responsibility and accountability.

  - Their culture or upbringing encourages this response.

- Why are some people aggressive? Because...

  - They don't know how to be assertive.

  - They fear appearing weak or losing control of the situation.

  - They need to dominate, win, and get their way all the time.

  - They don't know how to compromise, share, or support others.

  - They mistake aggressiveness for assertiveness.

  - They mistake aggressiveness for "machismo" or being "cool."

- They're rewarded for being aggressive.

- They don't know how to be responsible for themselves and responsive to other people.

- Why are some people passive-aggressive? Because...

  - They don't know how to be assertive.

  - They are angry but feel guilty about being angry.

  - They've been punished for expressing their feelings openly.

  - They're not sure their opinions, feelings, and needs "count" as much as other people's.

  - They resent people in power but are afraid of having power (responsibility) themselves.

  - They also mistake aggressiveness for assertiveness, and they can't allow themselves to act aggressively.

Have teens summarize the "consequences" of each response style. Ask, "What happens to the person who is consistently aggressive? How do other people feel toward her or him?" "What happens to the person who is consistently passive-aggressive? Are his or her goals ever really achieved?" The real problem with these response styles is not that they (or the person) are inherently evil, but that they make it practically impossible to have friends or an honest relationship with anyone. They leave all parties concerned frustrated, angry, and lonely. They prolong or create conflict and stress.

Then ask teens to think about the "messages" they get from society (meaning their friends, neighbors, families, and the media) about the value of being assertive, aggressive, passive, or passive-aggressive. Sample questions:

- How do television and movie characters tell us to act in relating to other people?

- Who are our heroes and heroines? Who are the "good guys" and the "bad guys"?

- Are men supposed to be aggressive and women passive?

- How is aggressiveness confused with assertiveness?

Explain that the role models around us may be giving us a simplistic, and misleading, view of relationships.

List the benefits of assertiveness. An assertive style of communication can lead to some awkwardness, particularly at first, and even change some friendships. Over time, however, assertiveness leads to:

- greater self-confidence and self-respect

- the potential for equality among friends, peers, family members

- better friendships, and more supportive friends

- a sense of control (sanity) over "crazy," difficult situations

- a sense that objectives and goals can be reached

- a sense of belonging to a group without sacrificing personal opinions or beliefs

- a sense of responsibility for self and others

- less free-floating anxiety.

You'll want to clarify that being assertive doesn't automatically solve every problem, change the world, or enable one to win every battle. Being assertive in an abusive situation, for example, doesn't guarantee that the other person won't continue to act irresponsibly. But it does increase the likelihood that conflicts will decrease. And it helps prevent the feelings of helplessness and anger from becoming overwhelming.

Suggestions for Other Activities and Projects

- As an extra project (or if time permits and everyone is so inclined), have participants complete the "Teen Inventory on Communication Styles" (pages 82–83). Respond with comments (if the inventory is used as an assignment). Or teens may wish to share their responses with each other in a small group meeting during this or another session.

. . . .

REFERENCES

1. Alberti, R.E., and M.L. Emmons. *Your Perfect Right.* (San Luis Obispo, CA: Impact Publishers, 1982), p. 13.

. . . .

RESPONSE STYLES WORKSHEET

For each of the vignettes below, identify which response styles are illustrated. Discuss why the behaviors might be classified as assertive, passive, aggressive, or passive-aggressive. What motivates each character to use his or her chosen response style? What do you suppose will happen in each scenario?

1 Two acquaintances, a boy and a girl, meet by accident at a restaurant next to school and decide to have a malt. When the bill comes, the girl stands up to leave without paying. The boy clears his throat and says, "Diane, I assumed that we would each pay for our own malt. I'm sorry, but I can't cover you today. Your share of the bill is $2.75."

2 An older sister has been promising her younger sister to return a new sweater she borrowed. The younger sister has asked for the sweater repeatedly, only to be told, "Don't bother me, it's coming." It's been over four weeks since the sweater was loaned.

3 Two friends are competing for the position of yearbook editor. Each wants the job, and they are equally qualified. On election day, they have ten minutes to present a final speech to the voters. One candidate announces that she is "much more experienced" than her competitor, who "couldn't design a yearbook or write copy to save his life." The other candidate says he'll do his best "to use his two years of experience as assistant editor to serve the wishes of the yearbook committee and the school."

4 Several teens are eating lunch in a crowded restaurant. Two are smoking, although they are in the "No Smoking" section. The waitress asks them to move to the smoking section. One teen gets up rudely and says loudly, "No one tells me to move. You don't want me, you don't want my business," and leaves. The other teen sulks, stubs her cigarette out on the counter, and spends the next five minutes slowly packing up her belongings.

5 Four teenagers are cruising around in one of their parent's cars, drinking beer. Two of them start to feel uncomfortable with the amount of drinking going on. Every time the subject of going home comes up, the teen who's driving says, "You're a bunch of wimps! This is our chance to have fun!" The group stays out until 1:30 a.m., when the driver decides to go home.

6 Two girls are at a shopping mall buying some blouses. At the checkout counter, one notices two missing buttons on the blouse she has selected and asks if she can exchange it for another. "That's the last one, honey," she's told. She leaves with the blouse, paying full price.

From *A Leader's Guide to Fighting Invisible Tigers* by Connie C. Schmitz, Ph.D., with Earl Hipp, copyright © 1995. Free Spirit Publishing Inc., Minneapolis, MN; 866/703-7322; *www.freespirit.com.* This page may be photocopied for individual classroom or small group work only.

Response Styles Worksheet continued

7 A small group of students is discussing the town mayor and his reelection campaign. Three of the four students are arguing vociferously: "You dolt! Only an idiot believes this guy is for real!" "You Democrats are all alike." "What's this guy's voting record, if you're so smart?" The fourth student is silent.

8 On their way to a basketball game, two girls are offered a ride by some boys they've seen around school but don't know. They decline by saying, "Thanks a lot, but we'd rather walk just now. Maybe we'll see you there."

9 A student is not looking forward to another year of school. His father expects so much of him scholastically, and has him signed up for all the advanced math courses. The student used to like math—but not this much. He starts the school year hoping that it will somehow be different (better) this year, and his father won't make him study so hard. In the meantime, he loses his father's calculator and is late to class.

10 A teacher finishes describing an assignment and dismisses the class. As the class files out, one student approaches the teacher, saying, "I'm interested in the topic you've assigned, but I thought you should know I wrote a similar paper last quarter. May I choose a related topic?" Meanwhile, another student in the back of the room slams down her books, throws the teacher a disgusted look, and leaves the room muttering, "If she thinks I'm going to write another paper on that stupid subject, she's dumber than she looks."

From *A Leader's Guide to Fighting Invisible Tigers* by Connie C. Schmitz, Ph.D., with Earl Hipp, copyright © 1995. Free Spirit Publishing Inc., Minneapolis, MN; 866/703-7322; *www.freespirit.com*. This page may be photocopied for individual classroom or small group work only.

TEEN INVENTORY ON COMMUNICATION STYLES

Use this inventory as a way to learn more about your communication and basic response styles.

1 The concept of innate human rights is one of the most important and marvelous constructs of a modern democratic society. Without a sense of basic rights, people cannot live together without destroying each other. Can you identify any basic human rights which you feel should be universally protected, which you would ideally wish to protect for yourself and others?

_____

_____

_____

_____

2 Describe an incident in which you acted assertively.

_____

_____

_____

_____

3 Describe an incident in which you acted aggressively.

_____

_____

_____

_____

4 Describe an incident in which you acted passively.

_____

_____

_____

_____

➡

From *A Leader's Guide to Fighting Invisible Tigers* by Connie C. Schmitz, Ph.D., with Earl Hipp, copyright © 1995. Free Spirit Publishing Inc., Minneapolis, MN; 866/703-7322; *www.freespirit.com.* This page may be photocopied for individual classroom or small group work only.

Teen Inventory on Communication Styles continued

5 Describe an incident in which you acted passive-aggressively.

_____

_____

_____

_____

6 Which of the above response styles is your predominant style?

_____

_____

7 Describe any benefits you've experienced from responding in your predominant style.

_____

_____

_____

_____

Any drawbacks?

_____

_____

8 If there is one person in your family or circle of friends whose response style is particularly troublesome for you, which style is it that they use? How would your relationship be different if the other person used a different style of communicating?

_____

_____

_____

Learning more about yourself and your response styles is critical for getting along with people, whether they are friends, parents, coworkers, siblings, or "enemies." It takes a lot of patience and thought to identify human rights and learn the positive skills of assertiveness that will protect these rights for you and others. Use the thoughts you've gathered here to become more conscious of how communication styles affects your level of stress, and the stress levels in people around you.

SESSION 8

BEING ASSERTIVE

Overview

This session builds on the assertive communication style introduced in Session 7. In theory, stress levels can be reduced as people learn to speak up for themselves, and speak to others, in ways that respect both the speaker and the listener. To start thinking and acting more assertively, one needs to know and feel entitled to some basic human rights—for example, the right to be respected as a human being, regardless of race, creed, class, nationality, age, or gender; the right to participate in self-government; the right to privacy; and the right to access to information gathered about us by others (including our government). Knowledge of these rights gives us courage to defend them and reminds us to respect them in others. In the first part of this session, participants therefore draw up their own "Bill of Rights."

Role-playing assertive communication skills is a good way to practice and feel comfortable using what may be a new way of thinking and talking. In the second half of this session, the ASSERT formula is used to help teens think through constructive, self-respecting, and respectful responses in role-plays that dramatize conflicts that violate some commonly held rights.

Overall Goals Relevant to This Session

After completing this session, participants should:

Experience the benefits of a range of lifeskills: physical activity, relaxation, assertiveness, supportive relationships, life planning, and positive "self-talk."

Feel empowered to care for themselves and seek help and support when needed.

Learner Outcomes

The purpose of this session is to help teens to:

1. Identify basic human rights they believe should be respected.

2. Identify steps in responding assertively.

3. Practice being assertive in a variety of situations.

Relevant Chapters in the Student Book

■ Part III, "Being Assertive" (pp. 83–99)

Agenda

In order to accomplish these outcomes, leaders need to:

1. Lead a class discussion and construct a "Class Bill of Rights" (15 minutes).

2. Explain the ASSERT formula (10 minutes).

3. Monitor small group role-plays in which students apply the ASSERT formula (25 minutes).

Resources and Materials

■ Handout of "The ASSERT Formula" (page 87)

■ Handout of "Assertiveness Role Plays" (pages 88–89)

■ Chalkboard or easel pad

Activities

1. Lead a class discussion on basic rights.

Quickly review some of the main points on assertiveness skills from Session 7, such as: a) their importance to human relationships, and b) the basic differences between passive, aggressive, passive-aggressive, and assertive response styles. Explain that it's difficult to be assertive if you don't know what rights you are entitled to, or don't believe these rights apply to you.

Ask participants to name some general rights to which they believe all human beings should be entitled. What are they? Ask them to construct their own Bill of Rights as a group. (You also may want to refer to the box, "Your Basic Rights," on page 95 of the student book.) This Bill of Rights should reflect the context of students' lives and their needs and feelings more than the rights of nations or citizens. Thus, instead of "the right to bear arms," they may wish to list "the right to having a voice in certain school rules and regulations," or "the right to honest answers from friends and teachers," or "the right to say no."

List these rights on the chalkboard or easel pad. Encourage some discussion and debate of the items and explore why the suggested rights should be (or shouldn't be) respected. If necessary, clarify the difference between "right" and "privilege." (It is our *right* as citizens in a democratic society to vote; it's a *privilege* to drive a Cadillac.) If students wish to have a right listed, ask them how they could protect this right without abusing other people's rights. Ask them whether their suggestions are attainable, and whether they are prepared to entitle other people to this right as well. If you have teens from another culture or nation, ask them to compare how rights in their society of birth compare with those in the United States.

2. Demonstrate the ASSERT Formula.

Pass around the handout, "The ASSERT Formula" (page 87). Explain that the formula is useful for learning how to think through an assertive response. When rights or feelings have been abused, people typically respond reflexively with whatever response mode they've adopted. They attack, withdraw, or think of a way to get even. The "attack" and "withdraw" behaviors are none other than our aggressive and passive response styles. The ASSERT formula interrupts the habitual response with a set of suggestions for constructing a better response.

As with any new skill, the ASSERT formula feels cumbersome in the beginning, but with time it feels more natural. Explain that each letter in the acronym stands for a suggested step in framing an assertive response. These steps should be taken in sequence.

A "A" stands for "attention." Before you can solve your problem, you first have to get the other person to agree to listen to you. Find a time, or place, or method which helps them focus their attention on you.

S The first "S" stands for "soon, simple, and short." When possible, speak up as soon as you realize your rights have been violated. ("Soon" may be a matter of seconds, hours, or days.) Look the person in the eye and keep comments to the point.

S The second "S" stands for "specific behavior." Focus on the behavior the person used that compromised your rights, not the person himself or herself, or else he or she will feel attacked. (They might get defensive anyway, but you've lessened the likelihood of that by depersonalizing your comment.) Tell the person exactly which behavior disturbed you.

E "E" stands for "effect on me." Share the feelings you experienced as a result of this person's behavior, such as "I get angry when...," or, "I get frustrated when you do _____."

R "R" stands for "response." Describe your preferred outcome, what you'd like to see happen instead, and ask for some feedback on it.

T "T" stands for "terms." If all goes well, you may be able to make an agreement with the other person about how to handle the situation in the future. Or you may "agree to disagree" or simply come to an impasse. Even if no agreement has been reached, you've accomplished your first goal, which is to assert yourself with dignity.

Generally speaking, its important to respond as soon as possible to a violation of rights, but it's not always possible to do that. First of all, it may take time to recognize that one's rights have been violated. People don't always realize that their feelings have been hurt. Second, it's not easy to think clearly when issues are emotionally charged. Third, it may be better to wait for a time when the other person is more receptive to talking with you. Sometimes it's appropriate to follow up a conflict with a letter, phone call, or conference. Sometimes the only way people can logistically make amends is later in time. Teens should not feel bad if they miss their first opportunity to assert themselves. Communicating needs assertively, even when it's done weeks later, can raise self-esteem and improve a relationship.

Answer any questions participants have about the formula, and explain that they'll be practicing it in the next exercise.

3. Monitor small group role-plays.

Have participants form small groups of three to five people. Pass around the handout, "Assertiveness Role-Plays" (pages 88–89), and tell teens to assign themselves the different roles. Each person should have the opportunity to practice the ASSERT formula at least once. To help the exercise get off the ground, circulate among the groups and answer questions, help settle role assignments, or rephrase the

purpose of the activity. Encourage the kids to be dramatic, to exaggerate the particular communication mode that's involved.

After letting each scene unfold for a couple of moments, stop the action. Ask the actors and the audience to brainstorm further possible strategies or scenarios for the characters. See how using the ASSERT formula would help the characters in the drama. Redo the role-play using the new suggestions.

At the end of class, summarize the activity by asking participants to report on their experiences. Ask, "How did it feel to be standing up for your rights? How did it feel to ask for help?," and other similar questions.

Suggestions for Other Activities and Projects

■ This session can be combined with Session 7, if time allows.

THE ASSERT FORMULA

"A" STANDS FOR "ATTENTION."

Before you can solve your problem, you first have to get the other person to agree to listen to you. Find a time, or place, or method which helps them focus their attention on you.

THE FIRST "S" STANDS FOR "SOON, SIMPLE, AND SHORT."

When possible, speak up as soon as you realize your rights have been violated. ("Soon" may be a matter of seconds, hours, or days.) Look the person in the eye and keep your comments to the point.

THE SECOND "S" STANDS FOR "SPECIFIC BEHAVIOR."

Focus on the behavior the person used that compromised your rights, not the person himself or herself, or else he or she will feel "attacked." Tell the person exactly which behavior disturbed you.

"E" STANDS FOR "EFFECT ON ME."

Share the feelings you experienced as result of this person's behavior, such as: "I get angry when..." or "I get frustrated when...."

"R" STANDS FOR "RESPONSE."

Describe your preferred outcome, what you'd like to see happen instead, and ask for some feedback on it.

"T" STANDS FOR "TERMS."

If all goes well, you may be able to make an agreement with the other person about how to handle the situation in the future. Or you may "agree to disagree" or simply come to an impasse.

ASSERTIVENESS ROLE-PLAYS

Role-play the scenes described below as people in improvisational drama do, i.e., by thinking through your character for a few moments, making up a few lines of dialogue that this character would be likely to say, and taking the scene from there.

Scenario A

A guy is pressing a female acquaintance for information concerning her best friend's love life. He wants to know everything about this friend—who she's dating, how often she is seeing a particular person, how "far" she typically goes on a first date, etc.

Guy

Your job is to badger the girl until she tells you what you want to know, or until she makes it clear that she will not reveal any more information. Secretly, you'd like to date this girl's friend, but you also enjoy a bit of teasing and the chance to spread a good rumor. You're a fast talker; be cagey, be aggressive, be "hard to say no to."

Girl

Your job is to decide how you want to handle this. You don't know this guy well, aren't sure you trust him, yet you have heard your friend say she thought he was cute. You want to protect your friend's privacy and are not sure how to get this guy to leave you alone.

Scenario B

A mother is getting increasingly concerned about the way her teenage daughter has been dressing. Particularly aggravating to her are the ragged, baggy clothes, spiked hairstyle, and nose ring. Recently, the daughter has been leaving the house wearing only a jeans jacket, although it's the dead of winter. One Saturday evening, the parents are entertaining a group of neighbors. The daughter sneaks down the stairs, hoping for a quick exit. Too late! Mother throws a fit right in front of the guests about her thin jacket.

Mother

Your job is to convey total exasperation and frustration. You've talked with your daughter so many times about her manner of dress, at least she could wear warm clothing. This time she's humiliated you in front of your friends, who were just discussing the lack of teenage respect for adults. You want your daughter to wear a sweater but you don't want to create a scene.

Daughter

Your job is to assert yourself without making things worse; your mother is likely to ground you for "insubordination" if you do. Plus, you're dating a son of one of the couples at the table, and don't want to appear completely ridiculous. At the same time, if you have to put on the sweater your mother likes, you'll die of embarrassment. How will you convince her you're old enough to make these kinds of decisions for yourself?

Guests

Your job is to decide whether to interject anything in the conversation or not. The scene is getting awkward. Should you ignore it, help the mother, or help the daughter?

From *A Leader's Guide to Fighting Invisible Tigers* by Connie C. Schmitz, Ph.D., with Earl Hipp, copyright © 1995. Free Spirit Publishing Inc., Minneapolis, MN; 866/703-7322; *www.freespirit.com.* This page may be photocopied for individual classroom or small group work only.

Assertiveness Role-Plays continued

Scenario C

Two friends are walking to class. One friend asks the other for a textbook that he loaned to him several weeks ago. The owner of the book needs it now to study for the geology exam. The borrower has unfortunately misplaced the book and doesn't know where it is, but is afraid to say so because the book cost a lot of money and he can't afford to replace it.

Textbook Owner

Your job is to become increasingly worried about where your textbook is. At first you want to simply remind your friend that you need it by the end of the day. When he answers you vaguely, you begin to get angry. If you don't get that book back, you'll have a very difficult time studying for the geology exam. (You could have asked for it back several weeks ago, but waited until the last minute to study.) Be persistent.

Textbook Borrower

Your job is to get anxious about confessing the temporary "loss" of the book. Your friend has a terrible temper. You didn't mean to lose the book—you don't think you did, at any rate. It somehow disappeared after the time you left the library to walk your girlfriend home. Be vague, inconsistent, and eager to get this guy off your back. You have your own troubles with the geology exam.

SESSION 9

TRUSTING RELATIONSHIPS

Overview

In Session 9, the theme of relationships and communication is continued with the goal of helping students "weave a bigger and stronger safety net" (support network). Friendships are wonderful buffers to stress, but they can also be sources of stress. The quality of friendship (more than the sheer number of friends) appears to directly affect our ability to withstand stressors and even heal from disease. Some research suggests that intimacy is empirically associated with health and longevity.[1] At the foundation of intimacy is trust. For teenagers, who are in the process of discovering new levels of emotion and need in their friendships, the concept of trust is tremendously important.

In this session, five levels of trust are defined, and participants reflect on friends they have known according to the five levels. In a group discussion, they analyze what makes a close friend trustworthy, and examine ways in which friends can abuse each other's trust. To close the session, teens role-play supportive responses to three scenarios involving common teen experiences with peers.

Overall Goals Relevant to This Session

After completing this session, participants should:

Experience the benefits of a range of lifeskills: physical activity, relaxation, assertiveness, supportive relationships, life planning, and positive "self-talk."

Feel empowered to care for themselves and seek help and support when needed.

Learner Outcomes

The purpose of this session is to help teens to:

1. Understand the effects of relationships on stress levels and well-being.

2. Classify friendships they have had according to trust levels.

3. Identify characteristics and behaviors of supportive friends.

4. Generate supportive responses to friends in need in three hypothetical situations.

Relevant Chapters in the Student Book

■ Part III, "Weaving a Safety Net" (pp. 100–110)

Agenda

In order to accomplish these outcomes, leaders need to:

1. Introduce the relationship between quality friendships and stress (5 minutes).

2. Lead a discussion about the five levels of trust and the attributes of supportive friends (20 minutes).

3. Supervise a role-play exercise in which participants practice supportive responses (25 minutes).

Resources and Materials

- Handout of "Trust Levels Worksheet" (page 94)

- Handout of "Role-Play Exercise for Relationships" (pages 95–96)

- Chalkboard or easel pad

- Handout of "Teen Inventory on Relationships" (pages 97–98) (optional)

Activities

1. Introduce the relationship between quality friendships and stress.

Friendships are like a two-edged sword. They can contribute to many unpleasant and anxious feelings: frustration, anger, doubt, and concern. They can also provide the most joyous of feelings: being loved, respected, and unalone. To draw teens into this discussion, ask them to briefly talk about the importance of friends in their lives.

To substantiate the connection between friendship and stress, you may wish to turn to some of the research being reported in various studies. It has been shown, for example, that when a spouse dies, the surviving spouse is at greater risk for illness and death. This risk is believed to be associated with the loss of an intimate partner. Other researchers who have studied people with chronic illness relate several positive outcomes with intimate friendships. Several controlled studies have found that seriously sick people, such as those with cancer, live longer if they join a support group.[2] In such groups, patients meet routinely to share their experiences and offer one another encouragement and affirmation.

Thus, we need to take the concept of a "safety net" seriously. It is more than a list of referrals to experts and helping agencies. It is not a trivial lifeline, but a substantive remedy or intervention for life stresses that may have as much, or greater, benefit to people as prescriptive medicine.

2. Lead a discussion about the five levels of trust and the attributes of supportive friends.

Friends come in all shapes and sizes. Some friends are very close to us, and others are simply good acquaintances. Many people are simply the familiar faces we see everyday on the bus or in the cafeteria. Not every friend has to be close to us, but we all could use a few really good buddies. We call these relationships "intimate," which can be a confusing term. Some people mistakenly equate intimacy with sexual closeness, but this is only one of its many definitions. The dictionary defines "intimate" as "closely associated." Perhaps the quality that contributes most to the intimacy we feel with our close friends is trust.

Refer the group to "The Five Levels of Friendship" on pages 104–108 of the student book. At the same time, distribute the "Trust Levels Worksheet" (page 94). Ask the young people to think about friends they have known, and how well they know them. Review with them the five levels of trust:

FIVE LEVELS OF TRUST IN RELATIONSHIPS

1 **LEVEL 1** relationships deal with facts. This includes safe, nonthreatening, objective information about activities or events in common (such as the weather, or homework assignments).

2 **LEVEL 2** relationships repeat, comment on, or gossip about other people's lives and opinions (but not our own). This is "they say" territory—which makes it relatively safe.

3 **LEVEL 3** relationships enter the land of "I think." Here we offer subjective opinions. The other person gets to know us from an intellectual perspective. This involves some risk-taking because we open ourselves up to possible conflict and rejection.

4 **LEVEL 4** relationships venture into feelings. We express feelings and experience feelings with another person. Since it's far more risky to share from one's heart than one's head, we become vulnerable and require more trust in our Level 4 relationships. If trust exists, we can feel genuinely connected with the other person.

5   LEVEL 5 relationships are those in which we can share our feelings about the other person and our relationship here and now. Level 5 relationships can't be forced or play-acted; they grow out of Level 4 friendships over time. They involve the most disclosure, the greatest risk, the deepest sharing, the highest degree of trust, and the most intense emotions.

Ask teens to mentally categorize where their friends and family members would fit in the above trust level scale. Reconfirm that it's impossible, and undesirable, to turn every friend into a Level 5. We need the 1's and 2's in our life, too. Ultimately, however, we need to develop the capacity to operate at Levels 4 or 5 ourselves, and to seek out other people who will perform as 4's and 5's for us.

Chances are, teens will know a lot of people superficially, but only a few really well. In the next part of the discussion, get teens to start thinking about why the level of trust among friends may vary and shift. Try asking questions such as:

■ Have you ever lived with someone for a long time, yet wondered if you really knew them? How can that be?

■ Have you ever found yourself surprised by a friend or relative—surprised by something they've said or done that seemed totally out of character—and wondered what they're "really like"? Why aren't people always the same?

■ Have you ever sat next to a stranger and, within a short amount of time, felt you already "knew" him or her, or could become close friends very soon? Why do you suppose that is?

■ Are you likely to tell some things to one friend or parent, but not to another? Why is that?

■ How much do you want people in your peer group or family to know about you? Why?

■ If you were on a remote desert island, how many people would you want with you, and why? Who would those people be?

Questions such as these lead to the general point that people often disclose different amounts of themselves at different times to different people. We often need to preserve our more private feelings for the few people we really trust. Those people are very special

to us. Other people we may have fun with, enjoy doing things with, but choose not to share much of ourselves with. Why is this? Perhaps it is because circumstances dictate a certain formality, or because we lack mutual interests. Perhaps we are shy, or feel awkward with people who look or sound different than us. More than likely, it is because the friends who are really close to us have in some way, through some shared experience, earned our trust. They behave and act in honest, consistent ways, and have supported us when we have needed it.

To close this end of the discussion, list on the chalkboard or easel pad the "Top Ten" characteristics and behaviors of supportive friends. This list should be generated by the participants, and build upon the prior conversation. What may be important to tease out in this discussion is the distinction between reasonable and unfair expectations of friends, and the meaning of "supportive." Is it fair, for example, to demand that friends carry your books to school every day for you? Is that being "supportive"? Is it fair to expect friends to take risks for you, or to act against their own self-interest? (Examples: lie to the principal to "cover" for an unexcused absence; demonstrate their "love" for you by having sex.)

2. Role-play supportive responses to friends in hypothetical scenarios.

Pass around the handout, "Role-Play Exercise for Relationships" (pages 95–96). This role-play can be done either in large or small groups. Essentially, this is an opportunity for young adults to practice the behaviors and attributes of trustworthy friends, as just identified above. The scenarios were written to illustrate three common kinds of "peer shock" identified by David Elkind.[3] These shocks are summarized below.

EXCLUSION

This kind of "peer shock" results from the experience of losing one's group, or being excluded from a group one wants to be part of. In childhood, friendships are formed mostly on the basis of physical proximity. That is, while kids may or may not like each other, if they live on the same block, or in the same building, they tend to seek each other out and play together. Age, gender, class differences, and racial differences are overlooked, and groups are as heterogeneous as the neighborhood. By high school, in contrast, teens seek conformity as a way to establish identity and feel psychologically secure. As this process happens, friendships can undergo drastic change. Teens tend to hang out with other teens who are most like them in terms of background characteristics, interests, academic performance, and physical attributes. As the rules for conforming to each group intensify, previous friends and would-be contenders can be brutally excluded on the basis of objectively trivial things, such as manner of dress or speech. Racism and other forms of bigotry are actually at a zenith in early high school.

BETRAYAL

The passion of adolescence is nowhere as clear as in the outrage teens feel when a friend betrays their trust. But because teens are able to think at a higher, more complex level, and are experimenting with ways to use friendships to establish power and build identity, they are capable of considerable deviousness and manipulation. In their excitement and need to be where the action is, they may play the field, saying "yes" to all invitations, and then taking the "best" one they can get—without even informing (much less apologizing) to the other people. They may express undying loyalty to the friend at hand, yet undermine the same friend when in the presence of another comrade. Expectations of friendship take a tremendous leap from childhood, when fairly basic rules of sharing and fair play were sufficient. Emotional needs are now part of the equation, yet the messages teens give about their emotional needs are not very conscious or typically well articulated. Thus, these unwritten rules for friendship are often broken.

DISILLUSION

Closely related to the sense of betrayal is the shock of disillusion that comes when teens discover that someone they have loved, looked up to, or idolized is, in reality, just another flawed human being. All the heroic, wonderful qualities that teens had imbued this person with—be it man, woman, girl, boy—sooner or later are tested, and the flesh-and-bone person is found wanting. Falling in love is something

teens do often, and do well. Learning to adjust that passion to human scale takes time and occurs through a process of disillusion.

HOW THE ROLE-PLAY WORKS

The role-play uses these common teen experiences as opportunities to practice being a supportive friend. In each scenario, one friend (Person A) approaches another (Person B) with a tale of woe. It is the task of Person B to be a supportive friend. As stated on page 103 of the student book, being a supportive friend entails the willingness and ability to:

■ honestly share what you are thinking and feeling

■ listen to someone without being judgmental or critical

■ be there when someone really needs you

■ offer positive feedback to others to help them see what's right about themselves and the world

■ ask for support, objectivity, or feedback from others when you're feeling anxious, vulnerable, or scared.

Suggestions for Other Activities and Projects

■ If time permits, or if homework assignments or projects are appropriate, consider having participants complete the "Teen Inventory on Relationships" (pages 97–98). Or have students write in their journals about the same questions.

....

REFERENCES

1. Moyers, Bill. *Healing and the Mind.* (New York: Doubleday, 1993), p. 68.

2. Ibid., pp. 157–176.

3. Elkind, David. *All Grown Up and No Place to Go.* (Reading, MA: Addison-Wesley Publishing Co., 1984), pp. 69–89.

....

TRUST LEVELS WORKSHEET

1 Level 1 relationships deal with facts. This includes safe, nonthreatening, objective information about activities or events in common (such as the weather, or homework assignments).

2 Level 2 relationships repeat, comment on, or gossip about other people's lives and opinions (but not our own). This is "they say" territory—which makes it relatively safe.

3 Level 3 relationships enter the land of "I think." Here we offer subjective opinions. The other person gets to know us from an intellectual perspective. This involves some risk-taking because we open ourselves up to possible conflict and rejection.

4 Level 4 relationships venture into feelings. We express feelings and experience feelings with another person. Since it's far more risky to share from one's heart than one's head, we become vulnerable and require more trust in our Level 4 relationships. If trust exists, we can feel genuinely connected with the other person.

5 Level 5 relationships are those in which we can share our feelings about the other person and our relationship here and now. Level 5 relationships can't be forced or play-acted; they grow out of Level 4 friendships over time. They involve the most disclosure, the greatest risk, the deepest sharing, the highest degree of trust, and the most intense emotions.

See if you can think of a friendship that exemplifies each level. Write that person's name down in the margin. What kind of conversations do you typically have with that friend? What do you do together? Finally, ask yourself, "What is it about the friendship at Level 5 that makes it work? Why is that friend a 'number 5'? What does that person do that puts him or her at the top of the Trust scale?"

From *A Leader's Guide to Fighting Invisible Tigers* by Connie C. Schmitz, Ph.D., with Earl Hipp, copyright © 1995. Free Spirit Publishing Inc, Minneapolis, MN; 866/703-7322; *www.freespirit.com*. This page may be photocopied for individual classroom or small group work only.

ROLE-PLAY EXERCISE FOR RELATIONSHIPS

In these role plays, one person takes the part of the friend in need, and one or more other people respond. There are three scenarios in all. Exchange roles or use different actors for each scenario.

The task of the friend in need (Person A) is basically to state the problem he or she is experiencing and to communicate his or her feelings about it. Person A must read the scenario silently first, and then proceed to retell the story to Person B in his or her own words.

The job of the responder (Person B) is to think of ways to react to the friend's problem. Responders should think back to the list made earlier in the session by the whole group of the "Top Ten" characteristics and behaviors of supportive friends. Additionally, they should consider the qualities of trustworthy friends that are highlighted on page 103 of the student book, *Fighting Invisible Tigers*. These qualities include the willingness and ability to:

■ honestly share what you are thinking and feeling

■ listen to someone without being judgmental or critical

■ be there when someone really needs you

■ offer positive feedback to others to help them see what's right about themselves and the world

■ ask for support, objectivity, or feedback from others when you're feeling anxious, vulnerable, or scared.

1. Excluded

(Person A should relate and elaborate on the following scenario, using his or her own words.)

You are just beginning the 9th grade. At the end of 8th grade, every student took achievement tests in math, reading, and writing. On the basis of your scores, you were put in the average 9th grade math section, while many of the kids from your old school were put in the advanced section. At lunch during the first week of school, most of the kids from the advanced section are sitting together. They are laughing and talking, looking pretty cool, pretty confident. You wonder whether to go over to their table or not. You know them all; you've been good friends with many of them since 6th grade. After hesitating, tray in hand, you decide to sit down because…"Well, there's no law against me sitting with them…they probably are hanging out because they got out of class together and naturally sat down next to each other." So you go and sit down. Immediately the conversation stops and a few knowing glances are passed among the other students. Then they proceed to talk in exaggerated terms about how difficult the math is that they're doing, how great they felt getting an A on the first quiz, and how awesome their teacher is—leaving you completely out of the conversation. You decide to go to another table and talk to another friend from your own math section.

(After hearing the scenario from Person A, Person B now responds. Person A should rejoin the conversation and dialogue until Person B has offered a number of supportive strategies.)

Role-Play Exercise for Relationships continued

2. Betrayed

(Person A should relate and elaborate on the following scenario, using his or her own words.)

You and your best friend have always done things together after school. When you were younger, the connection was around sports and hanging out at each other's house. Living so close to each other on the same block, it was natural to walk to and from school together. Since getting to high school, you've grown somewhat apart, because you have different interests. But you have always thought of your best friend as just that—a really good person who likes you and will always be around to do stuff with. Last night, you received the shock of your life: a third party told you that your so called "best friend" has been spreading rumors about you. At first, you just can't believe this is true. Why would your friend do that? After checking it out with a few more people, you discover it is worse than true: your friend doesn't seem to care that you know about the rumors. You call up the friend and have a terrible argument. You don't really remember what either of you said on the phone—you were too angry to think or hear clearly. All you know is that somehow your friend is "paying you back" for something you don't think you even did. You can't believe this is happening, and suddenly you wish your friend was dead. The next day, you walk to school alone. After school, you purposely find another couple of kids from the neighborhood and start talking to them about what has happened between you and your former best friend.

(After hearing the scenario from Person A, Person B now responds. Person A should rejoin the conversation and dialogue until Person B has offered a number of supportive strategies.)

3. Disillusioned

(Person A should relate and elaborate on the following scenario, using his or her own words.)

Ever since you could remember, you always looked up to your friend's older brother. He was the epitome of coolness. He used to be so nice to you when you were little, stopping to say "Hey" when he was riding around on his mountain bike. When he got his motorcycle license, you were the first one he gave a ride to, even though neither or you had a motorcycle helmet. You wanted to be just like him: smart, good-looking, popular. You wanted to have that big, magnetic smile that could make people swarm around you, just to feel the warmth of your grin. And that leather jacket! Now, that was really fantastic—something to die for. It must have cost hundreds of dollars. You kind of wondered how this guy could afford all the stuff he has; shoes, skis, a fancy class ring. Your friend (his younger brother) didn't have these things, and the two of them lived just with their mom, who worked at the grocery store and didn't have a big job or anything. How little you really knew this guy! Now the truth has come out: he's been dealing drugs for years. None of his teachers nor his mom knows; you're not even sure his brother (your friend) knows. But it's common knowl-edge among other kids at school. The "big" man on campus.... He still says "Hey" every now and again, when you stand close to him and get right in his face, but more often he acts like he doesn't have time for you. You really miss the person he used to be for you. One day, you turn spontaneously to some other friends and start talking about this guy.

(After hearing the scenario from Person A, Person B now responds. Person A should rejoin the conversation and dialogue until Person B has offered a number of supportive strategies.)

From *A Leader's Guide to Fighting Invisible Tigers* by Connie C. Schmitz, Ph.D., with Earl Hipp, copyright © 1995. Free Spirit Publishing Inc., Minneapolis, MN; 866/703-7322; *www.freespirit.com*. This page may be photocopied for individual classroom or small group work only.

TEEN INVENTORY ON RELATIONSHIPS

Use this inventory as a way to get to know your own thoughts about relationships.

1 **Do people really need other people? Why?**

_____

_____

_____

_____

2 **At what level of trust are most of your friendships? Are you happy with the number and quality of friendships that you have? How would you change any of your friends, if you could?**

_____

_____

_____

_____

3 **"Good" friends are believed to be especially good at things such as:**

- communicating their honest thoughts and feelings
- listening with an uncritical attitude
- taking the time to be there when someone really needs them
- offering positive feedback to help others see what's right about themselves and the world
- asking for support, objectivity, or feedback from others when they're feeling anxious, vulnerable, or scared.

Which of these skills seems most difficult for you to do? Why? Which of these skills would you most like to have your friends or relatives use with you? Why?

_____

_____

_____

_____

➡

Teen Inventory on Relationships continued

4 What are some of the benefits and joys you've experienced from having a really close friend or family member (i.e., a Level 4 or 5)?

_____

_____

_____

_____

5 What are some of the problems and difficulties involved with having a Level 4 or 5 relationship?

_____

_____

_____

_____

Learning to identify how close you want to be with people (how much you need or desire intimacy), and then learning the skills to foster that intimacy, are two of the most difficult things in life for teens and adults alike. Intimacy creates stress as well as relieves it. To be a good stress manager, you'll want to recognize which levels of friendship you've achieved with different people, and work toward adding more people or building on some of your current friendships.

From A Leader's Guide to Fighting Invisible Tigers by Connie C. Schmitz, Ph.D., with Earl Hipp, copyright © 1995. Free Spirit Publishing Inc., Minneapolis, MN; 866/703-7322; www.freespirit.com. This page may be photocopied for individual classroom or small group work only.

SCRIPTING THE FUTURE

Overview

Beginning with Session 10, we turn from the interpersonal realm to individual life planning. Perhaps the most difficult of all lifeskills to master is that of creating a personal vision for oneself, and then taking responsibility for turning that vision into reality. To do so involves a lot of introspection, risk-taking, trial-and-error learning, patience, support, and just plain courage. To become self-directed, teens need to first identify the "Big Decisions" in their lives that they want to be part of. To gain control over those decisions in a meaningful way, they will need to know who they are, what they value and want out of life. They also need to learn how to negotiate hurdles. This may mean acquiring certain skills and experience, learning how to get along with different kinds of people, or rethinking one's perspectives, beliefs, and attitudes. No wonder this takes a long time!

Session 10 deals with the first part of this process: identifying the Big Decisions and visualizing a future self. Session 11 provides a more concrete plan for identifying immediate next steps, barriers, and assets, and for developing a long-term outline.

By getting a handle on what we want out of life, we are really beginning to gain control over our stressors. Although "scripting one's future" does cause anxiety, living someone else's agenda (or worse, living with no agenda at all) is much more stressful, and ultimately unfulfilling. Fortunately, the previously learned lifeskills of relaxation, physical activity, supportive relationships, and assertiveness are all powerful tools that help with the discomfort.

Overall Goals Relevant to This Session

After completing this session, participants should:

Experience the benefits of a range of lifeskills: physical activity, relaxation, assertiveness, supportive relationships, life planning, and positive "self-talk."

Feel empowered to care for themselves and seek help and support when needed.

Learner Outcomes

The purpose of this session is to help teens to:

1. Identify the "Big Decisions" in their lives, and the people who have played a role in shaping those decisions.

2. Imagine what their future lives might be like.

Relevant Chapters in the Student Book

■ Part III, "Taking Charge of Your Life" (pp. 111–131)

Agenda

In order to accomplish these outcomes, leaders need to:

1. Lead a discussion on Big Decisions and Big Decision Makers (10 minutes).

2. Monitor an activity in which teens "script their future" (20 minutes).

3. Summarize the implications of taking charge of one's future (20 minutes).

Resources and Materials

- Handout of "Future Scripts" (page 102)
- Chalkboard or easel pad
- Handout of "Teen Inventory on Life-Planning Skills" (pages 103–104) (optional)

Activities

1. Lead a discussion on the Big Decisions and Big Decision Makers.

Introduce the discussion by explaining that the ability to take charge of one's life cannot be acquired overnight, and to some extent, it is a process that goes on our entire lives. It can involve several attempts and many steps; fortunately, life usually provides us with ample opportunities to take these steps and learn from mistakes until we get it right.

Explain that one reason it takes time to become self-directed and responsible for one's future is because it takes a while to see which decisions are "the Big Decisions," and to understand who's been influencing these decisions.

Ask participants to think for a moment about a decision or direction which is currently very important to them that either has already been decided or is in the process of being decided. This can include imminent or far-reaching decisions (e.g., curfews or post-high-school plans). Create a list on the chalkboard and have teens talk about:

- What is the decision all about—what is being decided?
- Why is that decision important to them?
- How will that decision get made—by whom, by what process, based on what factors? Has it "always been that way"? Has it already been decided? Or is the decision dependent on something?
- How do they feel about the decision and the process by which it is being made?

Summarize how sometimes teens have difficulty being part of the most important decisions that affect them.

Yet we all can learn from the experience of making decisions, even when we make bad ones. And making decisions is part of developing a view of oneself as an adult. Decision-making, self-awareness, and life planning all go hand in hand. Unfortunately, several things can get in the way of teens developing experience and ability in decision-making. Ask participants what seems to limit their role in decision-making, and list their answers on the chalkboard or easel pad. Help them see this question from a variety of perspectives. Possible influences include:

- parents who are overly directive; who have high expectations in certain areas of achievement or behavior
- inflexible school systems or curricula that limit options and demand conformity
- cultural, sexual, ethnic/racial, and other stereotypes that restrict visions for self
- powerful cliques at school that dominate taste, behaviors
- self: fear of failure, desire to please others.

Similarly, there are several resources that can help students gain self-awareness through decision-making and pursuit of personal goals:

- supportive parent, relative, teacher, or counselor
- supportive friends
- particular courses in school
- opportunities to try special classes, attend summer events, to travel or have experiences away from home
- self: through journal-writing or other modes of introspection.

Help students realize that there are, and always will be, other people whose influence or concerns will affect our life decisions. This is not bad! Many times we all need guidance, direction, a few boundaries to bump against. Having significant influential people, however, doesn't mean that we always have to sit "at the back of the tandem bicycle." We can learn to shape our own destiny.

Here is where assertiveness skills pay off; the so-called "Big Decision Makers" (such as parents and teachers) often have less power than young people want to believe. Most are willing to negotiate with teens as long as the teens are willing to assume some responsibility and are likely to grow from the experience. In the end, the most important decision-makers (with regard to their own lives) are teens themselves. Even the decision to avoid decisions and flaunt their anger or immaturity in adults' faces is a kind of decision. Kids are, ultimately, the people who will determine what they will end up doing. This doesn't mean that they have *all* the power to make *all* their dreams come true. They need a lot of support and good luck now and again. But in the end, each of us is responsible for choosing our dreams, and for learning how to pursue them.

2. Monitor an activity in which teens "script their future."

The purpose of this exercise is to give participants permission to start dreaming their own dreams: to be idealistic, to think beyond the confines of their present lives, and to center in on who they want to be and what they want to get out of life. What is important for them? As a way to begin working on this, they are going to imagine themselves as script writers, writing the script for a movie that tells some portion of "their" story. Explain that in this exercise, students should pull out all the stops—screen out all the messages from outside for a moment, and allow themselves to imagine the story of their lives as they would like it to unfold. Have them take out several sheets of paper and give them the following instructions.

INSTRUCTIONS FOR SCRIPTING THE FUTURE

In the next 20 minutes, I want you to imagine you are an accomplished film writer, writing to a studio executive who has contracted with you to produce your next picture. You've got a great idea for a film and you're going to tell him or her about it in a brief synopsis. You describe, in the first two or three paragraphs of the synopsis, the plot of the film. In the next couple of paragraphs, you describe the main character—e.g., his or her likes and dislikes, key beliefs, lifestyle, job, relationships, goals. There are only three rules for this exercise. First, the main character described in the script has to be you—as you imagine yourself at some point in the future. Second, the plot should focus on your future life (after you finish school), although it may reference your past. Third, the outcome of the story should reflect what you would most like to have happen to you. Be creative! Have fun!

3. Summarize the implications of taking charge of one's future.

When participants are done, ask for a few volunteers to share their scripts with the class. We recommend doing the exercise yourself, either the night before or with them, to share what your future script looks like. This provides them with good role modeling; dreams don't end, and grown-ups are constantly growing, too.

Next, present the handout "Future Scripts" (page 102) and have teens reflect on what they learned about themselves by scripting a movie about their life. Have them look over their plot and character descriptions for clues about their goals, values, relations with other people, work or career, and lifestyle. The great thing about visions is that they bring us energy and enthusiasm for life. The difficult thing is figuring out how to make that vision a reality. In Session 11, some of the steps for breaking down big goals into manageable steps are learned.

IMPORTANT

If you intend to lead Session 11 ("Planning for Change"), you'll want to collect the participants' scripts at the end of this session, since Session 11 makes use of them.

Suggestions for Other Activities and Projects

■ Ask participants to complete the "Teen Inventory on Life-Planning Skills" (pages 103–104). This can be used as homework, an additional project, or a prelude for a class discussion.

FUTURE SCRIPTS

What clues can you find in your movie that express your personal values, goals, beliefs? Look at your script for:

- experiences…journeys
- lifestyle choices…home…clothes…leisure activities
- career or job decisions
- other interests (intellectual, social, athletic)
- feelings…emotions
- friends…family…personal relationships
- successes…failures.

Answer these questions after reading your Future Script:

How is the person in the movie different from the person I am today?

_____

_____

_____

_____

What does the movie script reveal about me that I didn't really realize before?

_____

_____

_____

What is preventing me from pursuing and achieving this vision?

_____

_____

_____

_____

From *A Leader's Guide to Fighting Invisible Tigers* by Connie C. Schmitz, Ph.D., with Earl Hipp, copyright © 1995. Free Spirit Publishing Inc., Minneapolis, MN; 866/703-7322; *www.freespirit.com*. This page may be photocopied for individual classroom or small group work only.

TEEN INVENTORY ON LIFE-PLANNING SKILLS

Some people live predominantly in the past, some in the present, and others in the future. Right now, you're going to review your past and present in order to reflect on how to plan for the future.

1 Some people are natural planners. Others resist planning. What has been your experience with planning? Do you plan your time, your weekly activities, your courses or events for the new season or school year? Why or why not? If you do make an effort to plan these periods, how do you do it?

_____

_____

_____

_____

2 What are the key issues in your life—the Big Decisions that concern you currently, or have concerned you frequently in the last year? Who influences and/or makes these decisions?

_____

_____

_____

_____

3 Why should you work to identify your interests, values, needs, or goals?

_____

_____

_____

_____

4 How do you currently exercise some control in determining the outcome of these Big Decisions?

_____

_____

_____

➡

Teen Inventory on Life-Planning Skills continued

5 When you're 89 years old and looking back on your life, who do you suppose you'll hold responsible for the way your life "turned out"? Why?

_____

_____

_____

_____

Taking control of your life and managing it well takes a long time to develop. Total control of one's life is not necessarily desirable, even if it were feasible. (A life devoid of spontaneity and unexpected challenges and delights would be boring, to say the least!) One of the best things a person can learn is expressed in the Serenity Prayer:

> **Grant me the serenity**
> **to accept the things I cannot change,**
> **the courage to change the things I can,**
> **and the wisdom to know the difference.**

SESSION 11

PLANNING FOR CHANGE

Overview

Planning skills are powerful tools, once you have a sense of direction. They can help people change their lives. Even if you're not entirely sure where you are going or what you want out of life (and most of us aren't), planning skills are good "exploratory" tools. They can help you seek out information, experiment with change or options in a purposeful way, and structure what may otherwise be a highly stressful period of "not knowing." When people choose to structure their own growth, they are taking positive steps towards shaping their future, and in the process, they gain some measure of control over many foreseeable stresses—such as the need to support oneself, find meaningful relationships, and feel good about one's contribution to society.

In this session, planning skills are directly applied to the movie script drafted in Session 10. Plans for working toward the life described in the movie are developed in a cooperative learning group.

Overall Goals Relevant to This Session

After completing this session, participants should:

Experience the benefits of a range of lifeskills: physical activity, relaxation, assertiveness, supportive relationships, life planning, and positive "self-talk."

Feel empowered to care for themselves and seek help and support when needed.

Learner Outcomes

The purpose of this session is to help teens to:

1. Identify the connections between many small steps leading towards a larger goal.

2. Identify resources and constraints that can affect their progress toward this larger goal.

3. Expand the possible sources of support and reinforcement as they work on this goal.

Relevant Chapters in the Student Book

■ Part III, "Taking Charge of Your Life," the section "Writing Your Own Script" (pp. 119–131)

Agenda

In order to accomplish these outcomes, leaders need to:

1. Supervise a small group activity in life planning (50 minutes).

2. Meet individually with students at 10-minute intervals during the session, as needed/required.

Resources and Materials

■ Participants' scripts from Session 10

■ Handout of "Life-Planning Worksheet" (pages 107–109)

Activities

1. Supervise a small group activity.

Begin by explaining to teens that the process of taking charge of your life has two components: 1) figuring out what is meaningful, what one wants, and what one wants to be or accomplish (a personal vision); and 2) figuring out how to make that happen. Planning skills are what our analytical minds can bring to these situations. Planning skills involve different kinds of steps, as described below.

STEPS IN LIFE PLANNING

■ Identifying a piece of the vision that can be translated into a goal.

■ Breaking down a large goal into a series of small, related steps.

■ Getting information about the larger goal and the smaller steps that may change your idea of what you are doing, or how to go about doing it.

■ Analyzing current resources and constraints—in yourself and your environment—that can either help or hinder your progress as you navigate the small steps.

■ Outlining a timetable of immediate next steps.

■ Developing a support system, comprised of other people and yourself, to provide ongoing encouragement and incentives for staying on track.

■ Setting some benchmarks that will help you know if you're making progress, or the plan is working.

■ Developing "fall-back" plans, should your first options prove unworthy or unattainable.

Distribute the "Life-Planning Worksheet" (pages 107–109) and talk more about what the steps in life planning mean, why they are important, and how to go about completing the plan. You may want to provide one completed example, to show them how to work through going from a vision to a goal statement, and then breaking down that goal into a series of small steps, etc.

Explain that students will be working in small groups on their Life Plans and then meeting with you individually to ask questions and arrange for follow-up consultation or support. Divide the group into several small clusters. After spending some time creating their first draft, teens should stop and share their plans with others in the group. Each participant should get individual feedback from the other group members. Explain that the purpose of the group is not to compete, but to help each member think through the various process steps listed on the worksheet. By the end of the session, each participant should have at least one idea sketched out for each heading.

Remind teens about what was learned previously about communication styles and supportive networks. The idea is to offer constructive help in problem-solving—not to put down some other group member's desired goal or plan of action. Leaders can reinforce the group work by circulating around the room, sitting in on the discussions, and encouraging teens to come up with more ideas. Help them clarify their goals, map out the intervening steps, expand on possible resources, and be specific in identifying next steps. Ultimately, the purpose of this exercise is to give teens some sense of ownership over the decisions they need to be part of as they move ahead into young adulthood.

This type of cooperative learning may be a new experience for some students, but it can produce fantastic results. When several people put their brains together, the impact can be empowering, especially if a support group atmosphere has been established previously. The activity can strengthen a teen's problem-solving skills, but the work isn't over when an individual completes his or her plan. This work also activates the concept of supportive networks, and thereby enhances the probability that participants will be supported in taking charge of their lives after the course ends. Several classmates will have invested in the plan!

2. Meet individually with students.

Teens may need some individual attention with this process. Invite them to schedule an "appointment" to meet with you for five to ten minutes to discuss their concerns with you. If possible, use this activity as a project that can be worked on at home, and provide for some follow-up time with individual participants at a later date.

If you intend to evaluate the students' life plans, you may find it helpful to review the suggestions in "Evaluating Participant Projects" on pages 115–116.

LIFE-PLANNING WORKSHEET

1. Begin with the vision.

Take our your movie script from Session 10. Pick out one major goal, direction, decision, or aspect of this script to focus on. Examples: Choice of college or job; pursuit of a major hobby or travel goal; action on a major societal problem. Write down a goal statement by completing the sentence below:

"If there's one thing that I really like to do in life, it is to: _____

_____."

2. Map out some small steps that lead to the vision.

"What are some things that I need to do in order to make this goal happen?" "Who are the people I need to talk to in order to better understand what's involved with this goal?" "What are some experiences I need to gain?" "What education or other training opportunities would help me prepare for this?" "What opportunities for practice can I arrange?" "What groups do I need to become involved with?" Breaking down a large goal into a series of small, related steps means seeing the connection between your efforts, formal opportunities, and the accomplishment of mini-milestones. This is almost the hardest step in the entire problem-solving process, but it can also be most exciting as you begin to get a sense of the map. Although it's quite possible that the steps may change as you gather more information on your goal, try listing below a possible series of steps leading up to it:

a. _____

b. _____

c. _____

d. _____

e. _____

f. _____

3. Get more information.

Get more information about the larger goal and the smaller steps from people who have been there. List below people to talk to, library information to look up:

■ _____

■ _____

■ _____

■ _____

■ _____

Life-Planning Worksheet continued

4. Assess your resources and constraints.

What do you currently have "going for you" that will help your journey towards this goal? What roadblocks or potential barriers will you have to face? List below your resources, and then your constraints, along with what you can do to maximize your resources and minimize your constraints.

Resource	How to Maximize This
■ _____	_____
■ _____	_____
■ _____	_____
■ _____	_____
■ _____	_____

Constraint	How to Minimize This
■ _____	_____
■ _____	_____
■ _____	_____
■ _____	_____
■ _____	_____

5. Outline a timetable of immediate next steps.

What can you do about this goal *today?* _____

_____

What can you do about this goal *this week?* _____

_____

What can you do about this goal *this month?* _____

_____

6. Develop a support system.

List below the people you can enlist to help you stay on track.

■ _____	■ _____
■ _____	■ _____
■ _____	■ _____

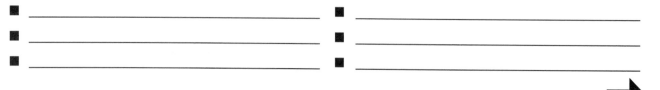

From A *Leader's Guide to Fighting Invisible Tigers* by Connie C. Schmitz, Ph.D., with Earl Hipp, copyright © 1995. Free Spirit Publishing Inc, Minneapolis, MN; 866/703-7322; *www.freespirit.com.* This page may be photocopied for individual classroom or small group work only.

Life-Planning Worksheet continued

Write down ways in which you can reward *yourself* for taking risks, accomplishing small steps, and persisting with your vision even when the going gets tough.

■ _____

■ _____

■ _____

■ _____

■ _____

■ _____

7. Figure out how you will know if you're making progress.

What benchmarks along the way will tell you that you are on the right path? List below some criteria that are meaningful to you that will make you feel like it's worth continuing on the path, because it is working / you are successful.

■ _____

■ _____

■ _____

■ _____

■ _____

■ _____

8. Develop at least one "fallback" plan or position.

Sometimes we discover our goal is not what we thought it was, and we lose interest in it. (Hey! It happens! People and situations change!) Other times, we realize the goal just isn't attainable. Write down one alternative goal statement, based on some aspect of your original vision.

"If there's another special thing that I really like to do in life, it is to: _____

_____."

POSITIVE SELF-TALK

Overview

In Session 12, we come back to the individual and the power each one of us has to moderate our stress. Nowhere is this power clearer, perhaps, than in the way we counsel ourselves. How do teens "talk" to themselves? What are they saying inside their heads as they see a tiger approaching? Have they learned how to give themselves encouragement, to calm their own fears, or to challenge their own dysfunctional coping patterns? Or have they developed negative, disabling internal voices, based on other people's low expectations or harmful messages? To survive in life, we all need to develop the sense that we can be our own best friend; we can nurture ourselves and provide wise direction. To do this, we need to identify the internal forces that prevent us from using lifeskills or growing positively, and to compose (and use) some potent messages to counteract those forces. An exercise to do just that serves as the primary activity in this final session.

Overall Goals Relevant to This Session

After completing this session, participants should:

Experience the benefits of a range of lifeskills: physical activity, relaxation, assertiveness, supportive relationships, life planning, and positive "self-talk."

Feel empowered to care for themselves and seek help and support when needed.

Learner Outcomes

The purpose of this session is to help teens to:

1. Identify some of the personal barriers they face in developing lifeskills.

2. Develop an array of positive messages to give themselves when dealing with these barriers.

3. Feel strengthened by the possibility of self-nurture.

Relevant Chapters in the Student Book

■ Part III, "A Short Course in Risk-Taking" (pp. 132–135), "The Burden of Perfectionism" (pp. 136–139), and "Growing a Funny Bone" (pp. 140–144)

Agenda

In order to accomplish these outcomes, leaders need to:

1. Lead a large group discussion on the value of positive self-talk (10 minutes).

2. Elicit from the large group three to five categories of internal barriers (15 minutes).

3. Monitor a small group exercise in which students compose positive messages for the different kinds of barriers (25 minutes).

Resources and Materials

- 3" x 5" index cards, one pack per small group

- Chalkboard or easel pad

- "Script for Affirmations Circle" (page 112) (optional)

Activities

1. Lead a large group discussion on the value of positive self-talk.

Begin the session by introducing the notion that the most important ingredient we have in addressing life's stresses lies within our own self. We don't need fancy sporting equipment, expensive health club memberships, and we may not have the luxury of perfect families, brilliant therapists, or extraordinary schools to help us. In fact, at some point in our lives, we may find ourselves completely alone with some very grave stress, and we'll have to figure out ways to support ourselves in order to keep on going. In the final analysis, it may be what we say to ourselves that makes the biggest difference in terms of whether we try a new lifeskill, take risks, grow. Do we tell ourselves that we can do it? That we can change, succeed, feel better? Or do we set up negative expectations of ourselves and of life?

Explain to participants that the power of positive thinking has been widely espoused by many psychologists and motivational speakers for decades. While some proponents can get carried away with this concept and imply that it has magical qualities (i.e., if you believe something *can* be true, then it *will* be true), there is no doubt that emotional health involves the ability to guide and nurture oneself. This means comforting yourself when something sad has happened, thinking through your anger, determining what is your responsibility and then doing something about it. It means seeing the good inside the bad, and vowing to persist. It means giving yourself the courage to try even if you fail, and the ability to learn something from failure. It may mean adjusting your standards or giving yourself greater latitude. It may mean believing in yourself, even when others don't seem to believe in you. The kind of message will vary from person to person, and will naturally depend on what we, as individuals, face as barriers to growth.

In times of great stress, we will need to serve as our own best friend, our own wise parent. Even when we lack a best friend in real life, or a wise and loving parent, we can develop this inner voice. One way some people develop this voice is by writing in journals. It can also be inspiring to read other people's diaries.

2. Elicit from the large group three to five categories of internal barriers.

The student book describes two different kinds of internal barriers: *fear of taking risks* and *perfectionism*. Write these headers on the blackboard and draw out some discussion from the large group about these barriers. Underneath each barrier, you might want to capture teens' definitions of the behaviors that go along with these barriers, and their explanations for why people have those barriers. For example, under "Fear of Taking Risks," you might list things such as:

Fear of failure...	been punished in the past
Fear of disapproval...	is sensitive to adults or peers
Seems too difficult	hasn't been challenged much in the past
Not interested, curious...	isn't used to things or people who are different
Don't want to be different...	knows there are penalties for nonconformists
Too stressful...	don't know how to moderate stressful feelings.

Ask the group if they can think of one or two other kinds of internal barriers—things that keep people from growing. Some possible categories are: locked into a stereotype; feel unworthy/inadequate; fear of the unknown; someone else is in control; apathetic; ultra-serious view of life.

When you have finished brainstorming about the three to five categories, divide the participants into the same number of small groups. Each small group will then choose one barrier to work on. (As an alternative, let people select which group they want to be in, based on their interests or needs.)

3. Monitor a small group exercise in which students compose positive messages for the different kinds of barriers.

Distribute a packet of 3" x 5" index cards to each group. Their task is to compose as many positive messages as possible. The messages should be written specifically with the barrier in mind that they have chosen to work on. In other words, given that barrier, what would you (or someone else) need to say to yourself in order to get you going? Keep up your resolve? Raise your spirits? The best messages will act on some of the feelings that underlie the behavior. Thus, a good message for a perfectionist emphasizes his or her worth as a human being, and not his or her accomplishments or performance. A good message for those who feel trapped in a stereotype asserts their right to be they want to be, not what others expect them to be. The group dealing with the "ultra-serious view of life" category might write some jokes and funny one-liners.

Participants can either write the messages collectively or individually. If they write them individually, encourage members to share messages with each other by passing the cards around the circle and asking for feedback. At the end of the exercise, ask one member of each group to read aloud to the large group all the messages composed.

The session can be concluded by laying out the cards in rows on three separate tables. Cards should not overlap. Tell the participants that they can go stand next to the table with the messages that they would most like to hear themselves, personally. Allow each participant the opportunity to select one card to take home with him or her.

Suggestions for Other Activities and Projects

■ An alternate closing exercise is the Affirmations Circle. Divide the participants into two groups of equal size. Tell the first group to stand and form a close circle, facing inward. Then have the second group stand and form a circle *around* the inner group. Each person in the outer circle should

stand about one foot behind the person in the inner circle, so he or she will be able to lean over that person's shoulder.

SCRIPT FOR AFFIRMATIONS CIRCLE

This is called an Affirmations Circle. Every person in the outer circle should be standing about a foot behind a person in the inner circle. Is everyone in place?

Now I'd like each person in the outer circle to put your hand on the shoulder of the person in front of you. Holding your hand there, whisper one positive, encouraging statement in that person's ear.

Keep your statement sincere, short, and simple—something you would like to hear, or something you think the other person would like to hear, based on today's discussion. You can use one of the messages composed in the small group exercise or think up a new one.

When you're through, stand back.

Now I'd like the outer circle to rotate one person to the right. Stop when you're standing behind the next person in the inner circle. Put your hand on that person's shoulder and whisper a positive, encouraging statement in his or her ear.

We'll repeat this until the outer circle makes it back to the beginning. Then the outer and inner groups will change places, and we'll repeat the process again.

When the Affirmations Circle is finished, end the class with a rousing ovation for all concerned, including you!

SUPPLEMENTARY MATERIALS

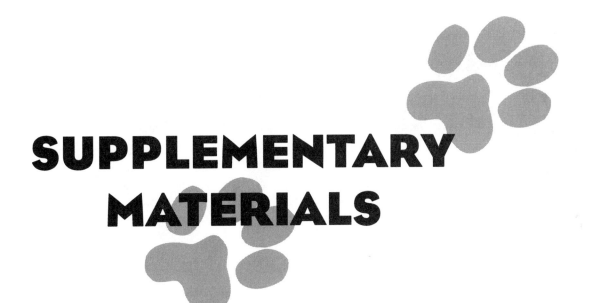

INTRODUCTION TO THE SUPPLEMENTARY MATERIALS

In the final section of this Leader's Guide, we offer a few suggestions and tools to supplement the twelve sessions. In addition to the two projects for participants described here, the "Relaxation Audiotape Project" (page 121) and the "Lifeskill Contract" (pages 122–123), you may want to consider developing other assignments, such as:

- a research report on the status of adolescent fitness

- an oral presentation on a book or film dealing with physical fitness, relaxation, or one of the other lifeskills presented in sessions 5–12

- a report on interviews with staff from teen crisis centers or hot lines

- an in-depth interview with an older role model (e.g., an athlete or business person), discussing how that person became successful and what he or she does to manage stress, achieve goals, etc.

No doubt your own creative spark has generated some ideas and exercises as well.

The remaining sections briefly describe the Supplementary Materials and guidelines for evaluating participant projects. The actual handouts and forms follow.

MEASURING EMOTIONAL STRESS

(Pages 117–120)

Emotional stress can be measured by totaling participants' responses to this questionnaire. Each question has a number of possible responses, and each response has been assigned a score. The lowest possible score is zero; the highest possible score is 74.

This questionnaire is a subset of items taken from a larger, statewide survey of teens in the state of Minnesota. The items are not copyrighted, and the authors encourage practitioners and researchers to use the questionnaire. The authors are also available for suggestions on use, including scoring and interpretation. Copies of the complete survey, as well as related monograph reports and a publications list, are available. Write or call: National Adolescent Health Resource Center, 1313–5th Street SE, Suite 205, Minneapolis, MN 55414; (612) 627-4488.

RELAXATION AUDIOTAPE PROJECT

(Page 121)

This project can be used as an adjunct to either Session 1 ("Recognizing the Beast") or Session 5 ("The Eye of the Hurricane"). It gives teens an opportunity to accomplish the following:

- demonstrate their knowledge about progressive relaxation

- design and create a tailor-made relaxation tool

- explore dramatic possibilities in script writing, recording, reading, and music.

Participants now know something about how progressive relaxation works, having experienced it in the group. There are many relaxation tapes on the market, and some teens might find these helpful. As they will discover in this activity, it's exciting and not very difficult to make their own tapes.

You might introduce the activity by explaining that because we're all individuals with somewhat different tastes, we may respond differently to various messages, voices, and relaxation sequences. Pass around the handout, "Relaxation Audiotape Project," on page 121. Explain that the point of this activity is for each person to make a tape that says what he or she wants it to say. By following the principles of progressive relaxation, participants can make highly personalized tapes that meet their needs and allow them to exercise their creativity.

LIFESKILL CONTRACT

(Pages 122–123)

This project can be used as an adjunct to any of the eight sessions in Part III: "Lifeskills." It is recommended in Session 6: "Getting Physical" as an alternate activity, but it fits anywhere in Part III.

The "Lifeskill Contract" gives teens an opportunity to accomplish the following:

- develop a plan for practicing a particular lifeskill

- achieve competency in that lifeskill by contracting with himself or herself and another person.

Pass around the handout, "Lifeskill Contract" (pages 122–123). Explain that the assignment is to select a lifeskill area (relaxation, physical activity, assertiveness, building relationships, life planning, or another area of choice), then prepare a three-to-five-page paper that outlines specific goals and strategies for achieving the goals. The handout is self-explanatory, so you do not need to say much more about it. Be available to give advice and feedback while teens are working on their contracts.

EVALUATING PARTICIPANT PROJECTS

We recognize that some of our readers may be in school systems, teaching these materials as part of a course. Others may have to assign students a letter grade for the course as a whole. For those readers who must assign grades, some guidelines on how to evaluate student projects and grade students may be useful. How you decide to evaluate these projects and assign grades will, of course, depend on your particular school and its evaluation system. But if we were

in your shoes, we would prefer using a pass/fail grading system, reserving "fail" only for the student who does not hand in final projects or has been a nonparticipant from the beginning.

Both the "Relaxation Audiotape Project" and "Lifeskill Contract" projects probably have their greatest benefit as teaching tools. Still, they will convey quite a bit of information on things such as:

- how aware students are of their stress levels and patterns of response

- how much students learned about progressive relaxation techniques and concepts

- how much they learned about their own values, needs, and goals

- how willing students are to take responsibility for their stress (for example, how willing they are to comfort or nurture themselves by purposeful relaxation, and how willing they are to identify and pursue individual goals)

- how well students know themselves (for example, how well they personalize the relaxation messages on their audiotape)

- how well they identify potent reinforcements for themselves in their growth plan.

Because our overall aim is to raise teens' levels of awareness of stress and use of lifeskills, you'll have to evaluate each student's final project individually in terms of progress made. As a rough measure, we offer the following criteria for evaluating the "Relaxation Audiotape Project" and the "Lifeskill Contract."

Similar criteria could be applied to the "Life-Planning Worksheet" in Session 11 as for the "Lifeskill Contract."

Relaxation Audiotape Project

1. **A personalized script.** Evidence that the student has (for example) selected certain muscle groups to emphasize (indicating that's where his or her stress tends to accumulate), or chooses vocabulary that is personally meaningful. (See the "Relaxation Audiotape Project" handout, page 121, for ways to personalize the tape.)

2. **Mastery of progressive relaxation concepts.** Uses techniques such as repetition; sequenced suggestions that flow in a logical fashion; calm pace; pauses; positive messages; having a beginning, middle, and end.

3. **Enough care with production to make the audiotape useful to them as a relaxation tool.** Consider whether the voice on the tape is audible, whether the tape is long enough, etc.

4. **Creativity and unusual care with production.** Examples: good use of music, special poetry added, the use of a special person to do the reading. (For extra bonus points.)

Lifeskill Contract

1. **Meaningful short-term and long-term goals.** The goals should have genuine meaning for the student. The long-term goal should reflect a personal dream or vision. The sky's the limit on this one, as long as the student is genuine (e.g., "I'd like to be president of the United States" is okay, if the student really wants to be president of the United States). The short-term goal should be ambitious, but more realistic about what can be accomplished by the deadline set forth ("I'd like to get elected to the school council," or "I'd like to attend the caucus of the political party I'm most drawn to").

2. **A reasonable plan for attaining the short-term goal.** By reasonable, we mean a strategy (or better yet, multiple strategies) that are implementable. (Hiring Michael Jordan to work with you on your basketball skills is not possible.)

3. **A reasonable measure of success has been defined.** ("If I miss two days of skating due to colds, that's okay.")

4. **Evidence that problems have been anticipated and tentative solutions explored.** There's at least one problem with every dream or goal; what is it? How should it be handled so the goal is still obtained?

5. **Evidence that resources, including people, have been identified.**

6. **Personal reinforcements have been defined.** Here's where a student's self-knowledge may be revealed. What works for one student (e.g., a special food or treat) may not work for another who needs a companion, or a schedule, or weekly meetings with a tutor or counselor, etc.

7. **Use of more than one person under resources, and especially thoughtful or creative solutions to problems.** (For extra bonus points.)

EVALUATION FORM: GETTING FEEDBACK FROM PARTICIPANTS ON THE SESSIONS

(Pages 124–125)

To improve your sessions, gather feedback from participants by using this evaluation form, tailored to your needs as appropriate.

LEADER'S GUIDE EVALUATION

(Page 126)

To help us improve this Leader's Guide, please complete this evaluation and send your responses to us at the following address:

Connie C. Schmitz and Earl Hipp
Free Spirit Publishing Inc.
217 Fifth Avenue North, Suite 200
Minneapolis, MN 55401-1299

We would be delighted to hear from you.

UNIVERSITY OF MINNESOTA ADOLESCENT HEALTH PROGRAM: MEASURING EMOTIONAL STRESS
Using Items from the Minnesota Adolescent Health Survey

For questions 1–14, check the box beside the statement that best represents your response.

1. How have you been feeling in general (during the past month?)

0 ☐ In an excellent mood
1 ☐ In a very good mood
2 ☐ My moods have been up and down a lot
3 ☐ In a bad mood
4 ☐ In a very bad mood

2. Have you been bothered by nervousness or your "nerves" (during the past month)?

4 ☐ Extremely so, to the point where I couldn't work/take care of things
3 ☐ Quite a bit
2 ☐ Some, enough to bother me
1 ☐ A little
0 ☐ Not at all

3. Have you felt in control of your behavior, thoughts, emotions, or feelings (during the past month)?

0 ☐ Yes, for sure
1 ☐ Yes, sort of
2 ☐ Not very much
3 ☐ No, and it bothers me a bit
4 ☐ No, and it bothers me a lot

4. Have you felt so sad, discouraged, hopeless, or had so many problems that you wondered if anything was worthwhile (during the past month)?

4 ☐ Extremely so, to the point that I have just about given up
3 ☐ Quite a bit
2 ☐ Some, enough to bother me
1 ☐ A little bit
0 ☐ Not at all

Measuring Emotional Stress continued

5. Have you felt you were under any strain, stress, or pressure (during the past month)?

4 ☐ Yes, almost more than I could take
3 ☐ Yes, quite a bit of pressure
2 ☐ Yes, some/more than usual
1 ☐ Yes, a little/about usual
0 ☐ Not at all

6. How happy or satisfied or pleased have you been with your personal life (during the past month)?

0 ☐ Extremely happy, could not have been more satisfied or pleased
1 ☐ Very happy
2 ☐ Satisfied, pleased
3 ☐ Somewhat satisfied
4 ☐ Very dissatisfied

7. Have you worried that you might be losing your mind or losing control over the way you act, talk, think, feel, or of your memory (during the past month)?

0 ☐ Not at all
1 ☐ A little bit
2 ☐ Some, enough to bother me
3 ☐ Quite a bit
4 ☐ Very much so

8. Have you been waking up fresh and rested (during the past month)?

0 ☐ Every day
1 ☐ Most every day
2 ☐ Less than half the time
3 ☐ Rarely
4 ☐ None of the time

9. Have you been bothered by any illness, bodily disorder, pains, or fear about your health (during the past month)?

4 ☐ All of the time
3 ☐ Most of the time
2 ☐ Some of the time
1 ☐ A little of the time
0 ☐ None of the time

From Blum, Robert, and Michael D. Resnick. *The Minnesota Adolescent Health Survey.* (Minneapolis, MN: National Adolescent Health Resource Center, University of Minnesota Division of General Pediatrics and Adolescent Health, 1986.) Used with permission in *A Leader's Guide to Fighting Invisible Tigers* by Connie C. Schmitz, Ph.D., with Earl Hipp, copyright © 1995. Free Spirit Publishing Inc., Minneapolis, MN; 866/703-7322; *www.freespirit.com.* This page may be photocopied for individual classroom or small group work only.

118

Measuring Emotional Stress continued

10. Has your daily life been full of things that were interesting to you (during the past month)?

- 0 ☐ All of the time
- 1 ☐ Most of the time
- 2 ☐ Some of the time
- 3 ☐ A little of the time
- 4 ☐ None of the time

11. Have you felt sad (during the past month)?

- 4 ☐ All of the time
- 3 ☐ Most of the time
- 2 ☐ Some of the time
- 1 ☐ A little of the time
- 0 ☐ None of the time

12. Have you been feeling emotionally secure and sure of yourself (during the past month)?

- 0 ☐ All of the time
- 1 ☐ Most of the time
- 2 ☐ Some of the time
- 3 ☐ A little of the time
- 4 ☐ None of the time

13. Have you felt anxious, worried, or upset (during the past month)?

- 4 ☐ All of the time
- 3 ☐ Most of the time
- 2 ☐ Some of the time
- 1 ☐ A little of the time
- 0 ☐ None of the time

14. Have you felt tired, worn out, burned out, or exhausted (during the past month)?

- 4 ☐ All of the time
- 3 ☐ Most of the time
- 2 ☐ Some of the time
- 1 ☐ A little of the time
- 0 ☐ None of the time

From Blum, Robert, and Michael D. Resnick. *The Minnesota Adolescent Health Survey.* (Minneapolis, MN: National Adolescent Health Resource Center, University of Minnesota Division of General Pediatrics and Adolescent Health, 1986.) Used with permission in From *A Leader's Guide to Fighting Invisible Tigers* by Connie C. Schmitz, Ph.D., with Earl Hipp, copyright © 1995. Free Spirit Publishing Inc., Minneapolis, MN; 866/703-7322; *www.freespirit.com.* This page may be photocopied for individual classroom or small group work only.

Measuring Emotional Stress continued

For questions 15–17, circle the number on the continuum which best represents your feeling.

15. How relaxed or tense have you felt (during the past month)?

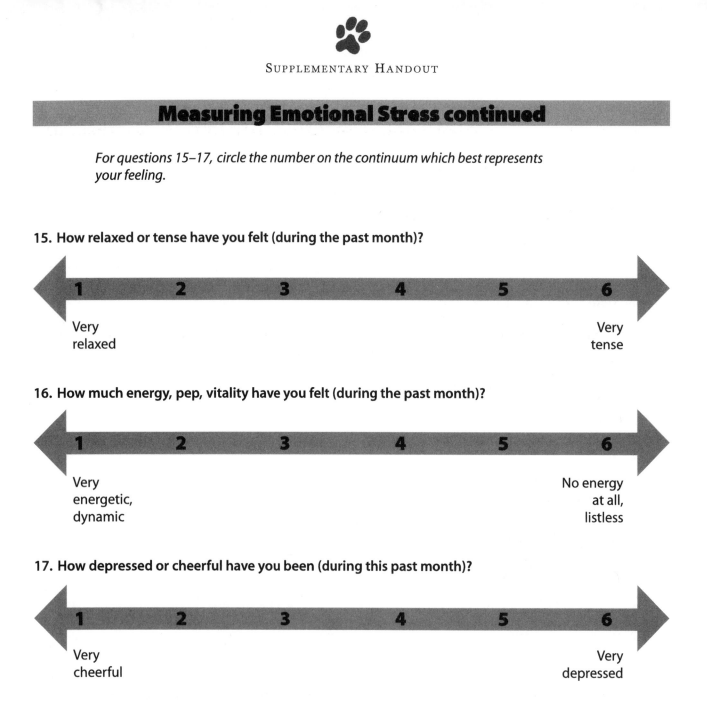

1   2   3   4   5   6

Very
relaxed

Very
tense

16. How much energy, pep, vitality have you felt (during the past month)?

1   2   3   4   5   6

Very
energetic,
dynamic

No energy
at all,
listless

17. How depressed or cheerful have you been (during this past month)?

1   2   3   4   5   6

Very
cheerful

Very
depressed

RELAXATION AUDIOTAPE PROJECT

This project is an opportunity for you to:

- demonstrate your knowledge about progressive relaxation

- build yourself a tailor-made relaxation tool

- explore dramatic possibilities in script writing, recording, reading, and music.

You now know something about how progressive relaxation works, having experienced it in class. There are a variety of relaxation tapes out on the market, and some of them may work for you. It's exciting and not very difficult, however, to make your own tape! After all, we're all individuals with somewhat different tastes, and we may respond differently to different messages, voices, or relaxation sequences. It's important for you to make a tape that says what *you* want it to say, and is read by you—or someone who gives you confidence—or has a particularly soothing voice. The assignment, therefore, is to make your own audiotape by following the principles of progressive relaxation as we've experienced them, but personalizing it for your needs. Here are some examples of how tapes may be creatively produced:

- Ask a favorite or trusted person to record your script.

- Write special messages into the script, such as reminding yourself to visualize a favorite location or season.

- When writing the script, choose your own metaphors and similes (e.g., "as calm as the lake on a still summer day;" "a wave of peace washing over me").

- Select a soft, relaxing piece of music to accompany the words. Make sure the volume is very low, and the piece doesn't interfere with the reading.

- Insert an inspiring poem or favorite saying.

- If you know that much of your tension centers in one part of your body (like your stomach, neck, or jaw), then emphasize that body part in the script.

- Experiment with different sequences of relaxation. Some people start at the top of their heads and work down; others prefer beginning with the feet and working up.

Tapes should be at least five to ten minutes long. A good way to make a tape is to record the script while a friend actually goes through the relaxation exercise. That will help you adjust the timing and pace of the exercise.

LIFESKILL CONTRACT

This project gives you an opportunity to:

■ develop a plan for practicing a particular lifeskill

■ achieve competency in that lifeskill by contracting with yourself and another person.

The assignment is to select a lifeskill area (i.e., physical activity, relaxation, assertiveness, relationship, life planning, or your own particular area), then prepare a three-to-five-page paper that outlines specific goals you'd like to achieve in this area, and strategies for achieving those goals. At a minimum, your plan should include the following:

1. Title and description of the lifeskill area.

In addition to naming the general activity:

■ list the specific activities within the area that you plan on doing

■ give reasons why you chose this area, these activities

■ describe your previous experience with or feelings towards this activity.

2. Long-term and short-term goals.

Be sure to include:

■ future or long-range goals that you'd like to accomplish in this lifeskill area (figure one or two years on down the road, or even more)

■ an immediate goal that can be accomplished in the near future (within one or two months, for example)

■ a target deadline for your short-term goal.

3. A definition or measure of successful completion of goal.

Describe the specific degree or level of success that you would be satisfied with.

4. A list of potential resources.

You might include:

■ key people who can teach, help finance, or lend support as you train

■ community resources for more information, professional or amateur groups, electronic networks (library, museums, etc.).

From *A Leader's Guide to Fighting Invisible Tigers* by Connie C. Schmitz, Ph.D., with Earl Hipp, copyright © 1995. Free Spirit Publishing Inc, Minneapolis, MN; 866/703-7322; *www.freespirit.com*. This page may be photocopied for individual classroom or small group work only.

Lifeskill Contract continued

5. A list of potential constraints or problems.

Identify any:

- personal limitations or roadblocks
- external limitations or roadblocks.

6. Tentative solutions to anticipated difficulties.

You might include:

- special types of reinforcement or rewards to use if motivation is lagging
- people from your support network who will hold you to your commitments
- other possible solutions.

EVALUATION FORM: GETTING FEEDBACK FROM PARTICIPANTS ON THE SESSIONS

Dear Participant:

Help me improve these sessions on stress management and lifeskills development by completing the questionnaire below. All answers will be confidential. Your honesty and constructive criticism are sincerely appreciated.

For questions 1 and 2, circle ONE number to the right of each topic description:

1. How valuable to you, personally, were the following topics?

		Not Valuable	Somewhat Valuable	Very Valuable	Not Applicable
a)	understanding stress	1	2	3	4
b)	progressive relaxation	1	2	3	4
c)	meditation	1	2	3	4
d)	aerobic exercise	1	2	3	4
e)	communication skills	1	2	3	4
f)	relationship skills	1	2	3	4
g)	life-planning skills	1	2	3	4
h)	self-talk	1	2	3	4

2. Was the amount of time spent on each topic the right amount?

		Not Enough	Just Right	Too Much	Not Applicable
a)	understanding stress	1	2	3	4
b)	progressive relaxation	1	2	3	4
c)	meditation	1	2	3	4
d)	aerobic exercise	1	2	3	4
e)	communication skills	1	2	3	4
f)	relationship skills	1	2	3	4
g)	life-planning skills	1	2	3	4
h)	self-talk	1	2	3	4

From *A Leader's Guide to Fighting Invisible Tigers* by Connie C. Schmitz, Ph.D., with Earl Hipp, copyright © 1995. Free Spirit Publishing Inc., Minneapolis, MN; 866/703-7322; www.freespirit.com. This page may be photocopied for individual classroom or small group work only.

Evaluation Form continued

Write your responses to questions 3 and 4.

3. Name three things about this class that were especially useful or enjoyable for you.

- _____
- _____
- _____

4. What suggestions do you have for improving this course?

Suggestions for topics:

- _____
- _____
- _____

Suggestions for learning activities:

- _____
- _____
- _____

Suggestions for assignments, texts, or other materials:

- _____
- _____
- _____

Suggestions for leader on teaching style:

- _____
- _____
- _____

Other:

- _____
- _____
- _____

Thank you!

SUPPLEMENTARY HANDOUT

LEADER'S GUIDE EVALUATION

Dear Leader:

If you have a moment, please give us some feedback on these materials. We're particularly interested in hearing from you if you implemented some or all of the sessions in this Guide. Simply write or type on a separate sheet of paper your answers to the following questions. Thank you.

1. Please describe your class and the young adults who participated (e.g., their age, gender, and other characteristics).

2. In general, how did you use these materials?

3. Which sessions did you use? Please indicate which sessions you used and comment on which you liked/disliked, and why.

4. In general, how would you rate the materials in this guide? Excellent, good, fair, below average, or poor?

5. Which sessions, or portions thereof, were most useful? What was good about them?

6. Which sessions, or portions thereof, were least useful? What was weak about them?

7. What changes, additions, or substitutions do you recommend?

8. What else can you tell us about the successes or difficulties you experienced when using this Leader's Guide? What suggestions do you have for revision?

Please send us a summary of the responses you gathered from the "Evaluation Form: Getting Feedback from Participants on the Sessions" (pages 124–125), if you collected this data.

Return your comments and suggestions to:

Connie C. Schmitz and Earl Hipp
Free Spirit Publishing Inc.
217 Fifth Avenue North, Suite 200
Minneapolis, MN 55401-1299

Other Great Books from Free Spirit

Fighting Invisible Tigers
A Stress Management Guide for Teens
Revised & Updated
by Earl Hipp
Proven, practical advice for teens on coping with stress, being assertive, building relationships, taking risks, making decisions, dealing with fears, and more. For ages 11 & up.
$12.95; 160 pp.; softcover; illus.; 6" x 9"

When Nothing Matters Anymore
A Survival Guide for Depressed Teens
by Bev Cobain, R.N.,C.
Written for teens with depression—and those who feel despondent, dejected, or alone—this powerful book offers help, hope, and potentially life-saving facts and advice. Includes true stories from teens who have dealt with depression, survival tips, resources, and more. For ages 13 & up.
$13.95; 176 pp.; softcover; illus.; 6" x 9"

Get Off My Brain
A Survival Guide for Lazy Students
Revised and Updated Edition
by Randall McCutcheon,
foreword by Steve Allen
This book has long been a breath of fresh air for kids who are terminally tuned-out. This revised and updated edition includes new study tips and strategies and a new chapter on using computers and the Internet. Readers learn how to combine laughs with learning, identify their strengths, refine their test-taking abilities, and much more. For ages 15 & up.
$12.95; 112 pp.; softcover; illus.; 6" x 9"

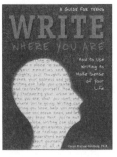

Write Where You Are
How to Use Writing to Make Sense of Your Life
by Caryn Mirriam-Goldberg, Ph.D.
This insightful book helps teens articulate and understand their hopes and fears, lives and possibilities through writing. Not just another writing skills book, it invites teens to make sense of their lives through writing—and shows them how. Recommended for young writers, English teachers, and writing instructors. For ages 12 & up.
$14.95; 168 pp.; softcover; illus.; 7¼" x 9"

Perfectionism
What's Bad About Being Too Good?
Revised and Updated Edition
by Miriam Adderholdt, Ph.D.,
and Jan Goldberg
This revised and updated edition includes new research and statistics on the causes and consequences of perfectionism, biographical sketches of famous perfectionists and risk takers, and resources for readers who want to know more. For ages 13 & up.
$12.95; 136 pp.; softcover; illus.; 6" x 9"

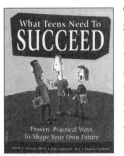

What Teens Need to Succeed
Proven, Practical Ways to Shape Your Own Future
by Peter L. Benson, Ph.D., Judy Galbraith, M.A., and Pamela Espeland
Based on a national survey, this book describes 40 developmental "assets" all teens need to succeed in life, then gives hundreds of suggestions teens can use to build assets wherever they are. For ages 11 & up.
$15.95; 368 pp.; softcover; illus.; 7¼" x 9¼"

To place an order or to request a free catalog of SELF-HELP FOR KIDS® and SELF-HELP FOR TEENS® materials, please write, call, email, or visit our Web site:

Free Spirit Publishing Inc.
217 Fifth Avenue North • Suite 200 • Minneapolis, MN 55401-1299
toll-free 800.735.7323 • local 612.338.2068 • fax 612.337.5050
help4kids@freespirit.com • www.freespirit.com

INDEX

BIBLIOGRAPHY

Ardell, D., and J. Tager, M. *Planning for Wellness.* (Dubuque, IA: Kendall/Hunt Publishing Co., 1988.)

Burns, D. *Feeling Good: The New Mood Therapy.* (New York: Avon Books, 1992.)

Canfield, J., and H. Wells. *100 Ways to Enhance Self-Concept in the Classroom.* (Needham Heights, MA: Allyn & Bacon, 1994.)

Chase, L. *The Other Side of the Report Card: A How-To-Do-It Program for Affective Education.* (Glenview, IL: Scott, Foresman and Co., 1975.)

Cooper, K. H. *The New Aerobics.* (New York: Bantam Books, 1983.)

Curtis, J., and R. Detert. *How to Relax.* (Palto Alto, CA: Mayfield Publishing, 1981.)

Davis, M., and E.R. Eshelman. *The Relaxation and Stress Reduction Workbook,* 3rd rev. ed. (Richmond, CA: New Harbinger, 1988.)

Hafen, B., and K. Frandsen. *Youth Suicide, Depression and Loneliness.* (Evergreen, CO: Cordillera Press, Inc., 1989.)

Hamilton, E., E.N. Whitney, and F.S. Sizer. *Nutrition: Concepts and Controversies,* 5th ed. (St. Paul, MN: West Publishing Company, 1991.)

Phelps, S., and N. Austin. *The Assertive Woman: A New Look,* 2nd rev. ed. (San Luis Obispo, CA: Impact Publishers, Inc., 1987.)

Rubin, T. I. *The Angry Book.* (Indianapolis, IN: Macmillan Publishing USA, 1993.)

Schmitz, C.C., and J. Galbraith. *Managing the Social and Emotional Needs of the Gifted.* (Minneapolis: Free Spirit Publishing, 1985.)

Simon, S., L. Howe, and H. Kirschenbaum. *Values Clarification.* (New York: Warner Books, Inc., 1985.)

Smith, M. J. *When I Say No, I Feel Guilty.* (New York: Bantam Books, Inc. 1985.)

Suzuki, S. *Zen Mind, Beginner's Mind.* (New York: Weatherhill, Inc., 1970.)

Travis, J.W., and R.S. Ryan, *Wellness Workbook.* (Berkeley, CA: Ten Speed Press, 1981.)

ABOUT THE AUTHORS

Connie C. Schmitz, Ph.D., is a program evaluator with a background in curriculum and instructional development. She received her M.A. in Curriculum and Instructional Systems, and her Ph.D. in Educational Psychology (Measurement and Evaluation). Currently, she is the owner of Professional Evaluation Services (PES), a company she started in 1997 growing out of the work she began during 15 years of service with the University of Minnesota. PES specializes in the evaluation of education, health, and human service programs that are funded by foundations or federal or state agencies. She is the mother of two grown sons and lives with her husband in Minneapolis.

Earl Hipp is a speaker, trainer, consultant, author, and president of Human Resource Development, Inc., a company that helps employees understand and grow through the almost constant changes in today's workplace. He has a bachelor's degree in psychology and a master's degree in psychophysiology. For four years, he was a clinical psychologist at a Minneapolis H.M.O., where he helped hundreds of people to better understand, cope with, and grow from the changes in their lives. Earl is a member of the National Speakers Association and is listed in *Who's Who in Professional Speaking.* He is available to speak to groups on the topics of his books.